CONTENTS

CRAFTING YOUR BUSINESS SYMPHONY
DREAM TO LAUNCH

THE POWER OF IDEAS

Understanding the Mindset of an Entrepreneur
In the rich tapestry of entrepreneurship, an

entrepreneur's thinking serves as the loom that weaves together dreams, challenges, and victories to create the fabric of success. It is a dynamic and ever-changing cognitive landscape, shaped by resilience, vision, and an insatiable need to innovate. In this chapter, we will delve into the inner layers of the entrepreneurial mindset, examining the psychological differences that separate those who dream of starting a business from those who make those ambitions a reality.

- Visionary Perspective.

At the heart of the entrepreneurial mindset is a visionary perspective that goes beyond the ordinary. Entrepreneurs have the ability to identify opportunities where others see barriers, visualizing a future unconstrained by the status quo. This viewpoint inspires their creativity, leading them to explore unexplored territory and challenge industry norms. Their daring belief in the power of their ideas is what converts a mere concept into a viable, successful enterprise.

- Resilience in Adversity

The path of entrepreneurship is fraught with hurdles, disappointments, and times of doubt. However, the resilient entrepreneur sees these challenges as stepping stones to success. The entrepreneurial spirit is defined by the capacity to weather storms, learn from mistakes, and persevere in achieving one's goals. Resilience is the key element that turns failures into useful learning opportunities, motivating businesses to adapt, evolve, and emerge stronger.

- Accepting Risk and Uncertainty.

Entrepreneurs shape their own fate, unafraid to take risks and negotiate the difficult landscape of business. The willingness to venture into the unknown, take measured risks, and learn from the results is a hallmark of an entrepreneurial attitude. The goal is not to avoid failure but to use it as fuel for growth. This fearlessness enables entrepreneurs to dance on the brink of uncertainty, transforming it into an opportunity.

- Passion is the driving force.

Entrepreneurs are driven by their passion. It is the driving force behind late-night brainstorming sessions, long work days, and transforming obstacles into interesting puzzles to solve. The genuine passion for their business is what drives entrepreneurs through the highs and lows, transforming work into a labor of love. This passion attracts like-minded others, building teams and communities dedicated to a common vision.

- Continuous learning and adaptation.

In today's changing business environment, the

entrepreneurial mindset relies on a dedication to constant learning. Entrepreneurs are avid learners who are constantly looking to broaden their skill sets, remain current with industry trends, and adapt to a swiftly changing environment. Entrepreneurs who are eager to evolve, along with an insatiable curiosity, stay on the cutting edge of innovation, propelling their businesses forward.

- Result-oriented Focus

While the journey of business is characterized by passion and imagination, the end goal is always results. Entrepreneurs have an unwavering passion to turn their ideas into reality. This results-oriented approach assures that every choice, pivot, and activity is focused on the ultimate aim of success. The capacity to reconcile ambitions with pragmatism and creativity with strategic thinking is what defines a successful entrepreneur.

Understanding an entrepreneur's attitude is like interpreting the musical notes that make up a masterpiece in the symphony of entrepreneurship. It takes a harmonious combination of vision, resilience, passion, adaptability, and a tireless pursuit of outcomes to turn ambitions into ringing chords of achievement. As we peel back the layers of the entrepreneurial mindset, we go on a journey to not only understand but also cultivate the attitude that transforms ambitions into profitable businesses.

An entrepreneurial mindset's attributes

Certain traits are shared by entrepreneurs, which help them see possibilities, take calculated risks, and persevere in the face of difficulty. Among these qualities are:

Entrepreneurs are motivated by a clear vision of their goals and a strong sense of passion for their ideas. Their drive and resolve to overcome challenges and realize their vision are fueled by this passion.

Creativity and Innovation: Entrepreneurs are continuously looking for fresh approaches to challenges. They question the status quo, think creatively, and don't hesitate to adopt unusual strategies.

Resilience and Perseverance: Entrepreneurs recognize that obstacles and failures are inevitable in the process of launching and expanding their businesses. They are resilient enough to pick themselves up after setbacks, grow from their errors, and carry on.

Flexibility and Adaptability: Entrepreneurs are

flexible and willing to change course when needed since they recognize that the business environment is always changing. They welcome change and see it as a chance to improve.

Risk-taking: Calculated risks are something that entrepreneurs feel at ease with. They realize there can be no meaningful gains without taking risks. They carefully weigh the risks involved and, acting on their analysis, make well-informed decisions.

Self-Confidence: Entrepreneurs believe in themselves, their ideas, and their abilities. They are able to overcome self-doubt and continue in the face of criticism or suspicion because of their self-confidence.

Resourcefulness: Creative problem-solving and resourcefulness are traits of entrepreneurs. In order to solve issues, they make use of their networks, mentors' counsel, and accessible resources.

Creating an Attitude of Entrepreneurship

Although some people may be born with some attributes associated with entrepreneurship, the entrepreneurial mindset may be acquired and fostered over time. The following are some methods for developing an entrepreneurial mindset:

Lifelong learning is important, so maintain your curiosity. Go to seminars, read books, and look for mentors who can offer advice and perspective. Accept fresh information and abilities that will advance your entrepreneurial endeavors.

Accept Failure: See failure not as a setback but as an opportunity to learn. Examine your mistakes, draw conclusions from them, and apply the knowledge gained to enhance your approach and judgment.

Seek Feedback: Assemble a network of dependable peers, mentors, and advisors who are able to offer helpful criticism. Seek out constructive criticism on your concepts, tactics, and performance in order to expand your viewpoint and enhance your decision-making.

Take calculated risks: Consider all available options and make well-informed choices. As you develop confidence and expertise, progressively improve your risk tolerance by starting with minor risks.

Develop Resilience: Resilience can be developed through self-care, coping skills development, and the creation of a support network to help one through difficult times. Resilience is an ability that can be improved and developed with time, so keep that in mind.

Establish a solid network of like-minded people who can encourage and support you by working together. Participate in business communities, go to industry events, and look for joint venture and partnership opportunities.

Establish Objectives and Take Action: Clearly define your objectives and divide them into manageable chunks. Achieve your goals by taking constant action and acknowledging minor successes along the way. You'll be more driven and concentrated as a result.

You'll be in a better position to handle the difficulties and unknowns of business if you comprehend and adopt the entrepreneurial mindset. It will give you the ability to think outside the box, take calculated chances, and persevere in the face of difficulty. By adopting this mindset, you may boost your chances of creating a profitable and satisfying business and provide a solid basis for your entrepreneurial path.

Finding and Assessing Business Concepts

In the dynamic and ever-changing landscape of entrepreneurship, the path from a dream to the launch of a successful firm begins with a critical step: identifying and evaluating business concepts. This key stage necessitates a blend of creativity, strategic thinking, and a thorough understanding of market dynamics. In this chapter, we will delve into the complexities of this process, leading you through a thorough investigation to help you find the most promising concepts for your entrepreneurial enterprise.

The Origins of Ideas:

A business concept frequently begins with an idea —a spark of inspiration that has the potential to grow into a profitable corporation. Ideas can come from a variety of sources, including personal experiences, industry trends, market gaps, and even unanticipated crossings between disciplines. We will look at tried-and-true ways for stimulating your creative thinking, helping you to see the world from an entrepreneurial perspective, and identifying opportunities that others may overlook.

Market Research and Trends:

A successful business concept is profoundly anchored in a thorough understanding of the marketplace. We will walk you through the process of performing comprehensive market research, providing you with the resources you need to analyze trends, determine customer needs, and assess the competitive landscape. By the end of this session, you will have improved your capacity to obtain useful insights that will help you determine the viability of your business plan.

SWOT Analysis:

Conducting a SWOT analysis, which evaluates the strengths, weaknesses, opportunities, and threats connected with a proposed endeavor, is an important part of appraising company concepts. We will provide detailed guidance on how to do a thorough SWOT analysis, allowing you to make informed judgments on the viability and sustainability of your business concept.

Prototype and test:

Moving beyond theoretical assessments, we will examine the role of prototyping and testing in the validation process. You'll learn how to turn your business idea into a tangible prototype or minimal viable product (MVP) and run real-world tests to get useful feedback. This iterative method helps you refine your concept and ensure it meets the demands and preferences of your target audience.

Ethical considerations:

In the quest for entrepreneurial success, it is critical to explore the ethical implications of your business idea. We will talk about the need for ethical evaluations and how your business can benefit society while avoiding potential problems. This section will assist you in developing a business concept that not only meets market demands but also reflects your values and societal duties.

Mentoring and Feedback:

No entrepreneur is alone, and getting advice from experienced mentors can considerably improve your ability to identify and evaluate business opportunities. We will discuss the significance of mentorship, including tips on how to form meaningful relationships with mentors and use their experience to enhance your business concept.

→   Coming Up with Business Concepts

Making a list of possible ideas is the first step in finding a workable company idea. Numerous techniques, including market research, brainstorming sessions, and first-hand experiences, can be used to accomplish this. The secret is to have an open mind and be creative, enabling you to investigate other marketplaces, industries, and clientele.

When coming up with ideas, it's critical to take into account your personal interests, abilities, and knowledge. About what do you genuinely feel passionate? What are your areas of knowledge and strength? Long-term success and happiness are increased when your business idea is in line with your interests and abilities.

Assessing the Potential Market
It's time to assess each potential business idea's market potential after you've compiled a list of them. In order to evaluate the demand, competitiveness, and profitability of each proposal, extensive market research must be done.

Determine your target market first, or the particular clientele that you think might be interested in your offering. Recognize their requirements, inclinations, and purchasing patterns. This will assist you in determining whether there is a market for your concept.

Examine the competition after that. Who are your rivals, both direct and indirect? What are their advantages and disadvantages? You can position your business idea to stand out from the competition by having a thorough understanding of the competitive landscape.

Estimate the potential revenue and expenses related to bringing each idea to market in order to determine how profitable it is. Take into account variables like cost of production, marketing, price, and possible profit margins. You can use this study to ascertain whether the concept has the potential to produce long-term financial gains.

Evaluating Resources and Feasibility
It's critical to evaluate each business idea's viability in addition to its market potential. Take into account the resources financial, human, and technological needed to realize the concept. Do you possess the abilities, know-how, and expertise needed to carry out the plan? Are there any obstacles pertaining to laws or regulations that require attention?

Determine whether each idea can be scaled. Is it simple to duplicate the concept or broaden it to appeal to a wider audience? Think of the long-term possibilities for growth and expansion.

It's also critical to evaluate the risks attached to each concept. Determine any risks, impediments, and difficulties that might appear during the implementation stage. This will assist you in formulating plans to lessen these risks and raise your chances of success.

Confirming the Concept

It's time to validate each idea after assessing its viability, market potential, and resource requirements. This entails getting input from stakeholders, industry insiders, and prospective clients to ascertain whether there is a true need and interest in your good or service.

To get opinions and insights, hold focus groups, interviews, or surveys. Inquire about the requirements, tastes, and willingness to pay of potential clients for your goods or services. You can improve your idea and make any essential changes before proceeding with it with the help of this feedback.

If you want to test the market, think about developing a prototype or minimal viable product (MVP). This enables you to get feedback from actual users and confirm the idea before devoting a substantial amount of time and resources to full-scale development.

You can more successfully find and assess company ideas by using the methods outlined here, which will raise the probability that you will choose the one with the best chance of succeeding. Recall that idea identification and evaluation are iterative processes. Stay receptive to criticism, make any revisions, and keep honing your concept until it's ideal for your entrepreneurial endeavors.

Carrying out Market Research

One of the fundamental cornerstones of turning your entrepreneurial concept into a practical business reality is conducting diligent and thorough market research. A successful business launch involves a thorough awareness of the market landscape, consumer behavior, and industry trends, just as a symphony necessitates the precise arrangement of several instruments to produce a harmonic tune.

Market research acts as the conductor of your company symphony, helping you through the complexity and nuances of your target market. This essential phase entails the methodical collection, analysis, and interpretation of data that will influence your business strategy, develop your product or service offerings, and eventually contribute to the symphonic success of your venture.

To begin this path of discovery, first select your

target audience. Understand the demographics, psychographics, and behavioral patterns of the people or organizations that your company intends to serve. Dive into your target consumers' minds with surveys, interviews, and observation to discover their wants, preferences, and problem spots. This detailed understanding will provide the framework for a product or service that resonates well with your target market.

In the delicate ballet of market research, competitor analysis gets the spotlight. Just as musicians study their colleagues' techniques, businesses must examine the strengths and limitations of existing market participants. Determine your competitors' offerings, pricing plans, and marketing tactics. This not only provides insights into potential market gaps, but it also allows you to fine-tune your own approach, ensuring that your company stands out as a distinct and enticing option.

As you navigate the orchestra of market dynamics, don't forget to look into macroeconomic issues that could affect your firm. Economic developments, regulatory changes, and technological advancements all have a significant impact on your business. Stay tuned to these external variables so you can anticipate market developments and adjust your business plan accordingly.

Market research is a dynamic process that

necessitates ongoing attention and adaptability. Use both primary and secondary research approaches to collect data, taking advantage of the plethora of information available through web sites, industry studies, and expert opinions. Stay in touch with your audience via social media, forums, and other means to stay informed about their changing tastes and behaviors.

Recognizing the Value of Market Research

You can gain a thorough grasp of your target market's requirements, preferences, and behaviors by conducting market research. It assists you in recognizing market opportunities and obstacles, enabling you to efficiently customize your goods or services to satisfy consumer wants. You can create marketing tactics that connect with your audience and set your company apart from rivals by having a thorough understanding of your target market.

Clarifying Your Study Goals

Establishing your research objectives is crucial before you begin any market research. What particular details are you looking to collect? Do you want to know about market size, competitive analysis, or consumer preferences? Your research efforts will be guided, and the proper data will be gathered so that you can draw well-informed conclusions if your research objectives are well defined.

Differentiating Between Primary and Secondary Study Techniques

Fundamental and secondary research are the two fundamental categories of market research methodologies.

Gathering information directly from your target market is known as primary research. Surveys, interviews, focus groups, and observations can all be used for this. Primary research gives you access to first-hand knowledge that is unique to your company and enables you to get direct feedback from prospective clients.

On the other hand, secondary research entails compiling previously published data and information from a range of sources, including web databases, government publications, and industry reports. You can gain a deeper comprehension of the market, industry trends, and competitor analysis by conducting secondary research. Although it is less expensive than primary research, it could not be as customized to your particular business needs.

Performing a Primary Study

It's crucial to plan your research methodology when doing primary research in order to collect the most precise and pertinent data possible. Utilizing surveys to get quantitative data from a large number of respondents can be rather successful. Your target audience can receive paper surveys or ones you create online. You can collect qualitative information and learn more about the ideas, opinions, and experiences of your potential clients by holding focus groups and conducting interviews.

Make sure to include open-ended questions in your surveys, interviews, or focus groups to encourage participants to give thorough responses. This will assist you in gaining insightful knowledge and comprehending the underlying desires and motivations of your target market.

Data Analysis and Interpretation

It's time to evaluate and understand the data after you've gathered it. To do this, the data must be arranged, patterns and trends must be found, and insightful conclusions must be drawn. To examine numerical data and find trends or correlations, use statistical analysis tools or software. Thematic analysis is a useful tool for identifying common themes or patterns in responses to qualitative data.

Critical thinking and the capacity to derive practical insights are necessary for data interpretation. Utilize the opportunities and difficulties that the data presents to help you fine-tune your business plan. You can modify your marketing and product development strategy, for instance, if your research indicates a market gap that your offering can close.

Gaining an Understanding of Rival Analysis

The analysis of competitors is a crucial part of market research. It entails determining and assessing the advantages, disadvantages, tactics, and positioning of your rivals in the market. Knowing your rivals will help you spot areas where your company can stand out from the crowd and create plans to give you an edge.

Finding your direct and indirect competitors is the first step in conducting a competitor analysis. While indirect competitors could provide different answers to the same client needs, direct competitors sell comparable goods and services to the same target market. Examine their price, distribution methods, marketing approaches, and client testimonials. This will assist you in figuring out how to market your company and differentiate yourself from the competition.

Maintaining Current Market Trends

Market research is a continuous undertaking. It's critical to be abreast of the most recent advancements in the market, the industry, and consumer preferences. To stay updated, go to conferences and trade exhibitions, read relevant blogs and social media profiles, and subscribe to industry newsletters. Being ahead of the curve allows you to modify your business plans and take advantage of new opportunities.

In summary

One of the most important things you can do to develop your business idea is market research. It gives you useful information about your target market, rivals, and market trends. You may effectively meet the demands of your clients by developing products or services that are tailored to their requirements and preferences. You may improve your company plan and obtain a competitive edge by doing market research to find possibilities and obstacles. Maintain your dedication to continuous market research to make sure your company succeeds in the long run.

Examining Your Idea

In the broad canvas of entrepreneurship, where dreams take flight and enterprises blossom as symphonies of creativity, the critical first step is to examine your idea. This critical phase establishes the framework for the entire entrepreneurial journey, necessitating careful study, painstaking analysis, and an unrelenting devotion to making your vision a reality.

Every successful endeavor begins with the seed of an idea, which is then nurtured into fruition. As you embark on the thrilling road of turning your aspirations into a concrete business, the first act begins with a comprehensive study of the notion that feeds your passion and sparks the entrepreneur within you.

The assessment process goes beyond a cursory glance; it entails delving deeply into the complexities of your idea, dissecting its components, uncovering its potential, and determining its feasibility in the dynamic marketplace. Consider this period to be the laboratory of your entrepreneurial effort, where you wear both the hats of scientist and artist, methodically studying, testing, and shaping the raw material of your idea.

Begin by questioning the fundamental core of your notion. What is the problem it solves? How does it respond to a market need or desire? Understanding the significance of your idea is analogous to decoding the musical notes that comprise a symphony; each part must complement the others to produce a cohesive and resonant composition.

As you go further, consider the distinctiveness of your proposition. Is your proposal a new melody in a world full of old songs, or does it present a novel and inventive arrangement? Discover the unique characteristics that distinguish your project, transforming it from just another company venture to a composition that stands out in the big symphony of entrepreneurship.

The inspection method should also include a thorough market investigation. Explore the environment in which your concept will thrive —define your target audience, analyze rivals, and uncover trends that may influence the course of your business. This market symphony necessitates a strong ear for nuances and an acute eye for patterns, which will guide you to make informed decisions that are in sync with the pulse of your potential clients.

Consider the scalability and durability of your idea. Your business concept, like a musical piece, should be adaptable and grow with time. Anticipate potential problems and devise solutions to overcome them, ensuring that your entrepreneurial symphony survives the test of time.

Accepting input becomes increasingly important during this stage. Seek feedback from mentors, peers, and potential consumers, treating their views as valuable notes that add to the richness of your composition. Constructive criticism is the process of honing a raw concept into a polished gem.

The study of your idea is not a static checkpoint but rather a dynamic process that evolves as you collect insights and knowledge. It's a symphonic inquiry, with each note adding to the melody of your entrepreneurial journey. As you methodically explore your idea, you lay the groundwork for the crescendo of success that lies ahead, transforming your business aspirations into a symphony that echoes across the entrepreneurial landscape.

Realizing Concept Validation's Significance

Concept validation is an essential phase in the entrepreneurial process that aids in determining the viability and feasibility of your company idea. You may reduce the risks involved in starting a new business and improve your chances of success by having your idea validated. For the following main reasons, concept validation is essential:

Risk Mitigation: Before devoting substantial resources to your idea, you can find and fix any possible bugs or weaknesses by validating your ideas. You may reduce risks and make well-informed decisions if you are aware of market demand and possible obstacles.

Saving Time and Resources: You may prevent squandering time and money on concepts that might not have a market or client need by verifying your idea early on. It assists you in concentrating your attention on concepts with a better chance of succeeding.

Increasing Confidence: Having your idea validated gives you the knowledge that it has the potential to be successful. It provides you with the assurance you require to proceed with fervor and conviction.

Researching the Market

One of the most important steps in concept validation is market research. It entails obtaining and examining data regarding your target market, rivals, and market trends. The following are essential measures for carrying out efficient market research:

Identify the market you want to reach:
Determine the particular demographic or industry your product or service is intended to cater to. Recognize their needs, pain points, preferences, and demographics.

Examine the Competitive Environment: Find out about the advantages, disadvantages, and market positioning of your rivals by conducting research and analysis. Determine any holes or openings that your idea can take advantage of.

Determine Market Trends: Keep abreast of the most recent developments and trends in the market. This will assist you in comprehending the dynamics of the market and modifying your concept as necessary.

Obtain Customer Input: Talk to prospective clients to get their opinions on your idea. To learn about their requirements, preferences, and readiness to pay for your good or service, hold focus groups, surveys, or interviews.

Minimum Viable Product (MVP) and prototyping
Creating a Minimum Viable Product (MVP) and conducting prototyping are efficient methods to

further validate your idea. A prototype is an early iteration of your good or service that lets you evaluate its performance and get user input. In contrast, an MVP is a condensed version of your product or service that only has the essential functionality required to address the issue at hand.

Prototyping: Make a working prototype that highlights the salient characteristics and advantages of your good or service. This could be a digital mockup, a wireframe, or a real prototype. Get input on the prototype from possible clients, financiers, or business authorities.

Minimum Viable Product (MVP): Create an MVP that highlights the main selling point of your idea. The MVP ought to be sufficiently functional to address the issue and obtain practical input. Introduce the MVP to a small sample of early adopters, and use their input to improve and hone your product.

Validating and Reworking Your Idea
Iterating and testing your concept is a continuous process that lets you hone and polish it in response to feedback from the real world. The following are essential actions to take in order to test and refine your idea:

Establish Specific Goals: Prioritize your goals and KPIs so that testing and iteration may help you reach them. User engagement measurements, revenue targets, and customer acquisition are a few examples of this.

Collect Feedback: Get input from stakeholders, consumers, and your target market on a regular basis. Surveys, interviews, usability testing, and data analysis on user behavior can all be used to achieve this.

Analyze and iterate: Examine the data and comments received to determine what needs to be improved. Make iterative adjustments to your concept, product, or service using the information provided here. This can entail improving the user experience, changing the price, or improving the features.

Analyze Outcomes: Consistently assess and gauge the success of your revisions. Determine whether the modifications have improved revenue, customer satisfaction, or other important performance metrics.

You may improve your offering, validate your concept, and raise your chances of creating a long-lasting, profitable company by following these steps. Recall that idea validation is a continuous process that ought to carry on long after your business has launched. To remain ahead in the highly competitive landscape, have an open mind, adjust to changes in the industry, and never stop innovating.

CRAFTING A SOLID BUSINESS PLAN

Clarifying Your Goals and Vision

A clear vision and mission that direct your actions and decisions are essential for developing a successful firm. Your mission statement outlines the goals and principles that guide your company, whereas your vision statement depicts the ideal future you hope to realize. Establishing your vision and mission will give you a sense of purpose and direction. It will also work as a compass to help you align your team and draw in clients that share your values.

2.1.1 Creating Your Vision

Your vision is the ultimate goal you have for your company. It paints a clear and motivating image of your long-term goals. Thinking broadly and visualizing the impact you want your company to make on the world are essential for creating a compelling vision. The following actions will assist you in defining your vision:

Consider your purpose and passion. Begin by asking yourself why you initially decided to launch this company. What issue are you trying to resolve? Which effect are you hoping to achieve? Developing a vision that matters to you and your stakeholders will be easier if you know what your passion and purpose are.

Think about the future. Consider the state of your company after five, ten, or even twenty years. Consider the markets you will serve, the size of your activities, and the value you will provide. Imagine the good that your company will accomplish for the world.

Make it ambitious and inspiring. Your vision needs to be aspirational enough to spur you and your group to action. It should test your limits and encourage you to think creatively. Strive toward an aspirational but attainable goal using the appropriate tactics and tools.

Make it memorable and succinct. Write a vision statement that is clear and simple to recall. Make use of concise, impactful language that expresses the core of your idea. Steer clear of technical terms or jargon that could confuse listeners or lessen the impact of your message.

2.1.2 Clarifying Your Purpose

Your mission statement outlines the current goals and core values of your company, but its vision statement speaks to the future. It describes the precise steps you'll take to realize your vision as well as the guiding ideas that will influence your choices. The following actions will assist you in defining your mission:

Determine who your intended audience is. Recognize your target audience's demands and preferences before anything else. How you will service and add value for your clients should be the focus of your mission statement.

Describe the special value that you offer. Find out what makes your company unique among the competition. What special goods, services, or encounters do you provide? Your unique selling proposition and the value you provide the market should be reflected in your mission statement.

Describe your core values: Decide which core values will influence the culture and operations of your company. These principles ought to guide your decisions and be consistent with your personal convictions. Customer-centricity, sustainability, innovation, and honesty are a few examples of fundamental principles.

Make it quantifiable and actionable. Your mission should outline a clear course of action for realizing your goal. It should include a description of the precise aims and objectives you want to pursue as well as the success indicators you'll employ.

2.1.3 Harmonizing Your Objective and Vision

It's critical to make sure your vision and purpose are interwoven into every facet of your organization after you've established them. To bring your vision and mission into alignment, use these strategies:

Share your vision and mission with your staff, stakeholders, and clients by communicating with them. Express your company's mission and core beliefs in a clear and concise manner. This will encourage others to accompany you on your path and foster a feeling of shared purpose.

Integrate your goals and objectives into your culture. Embrace your goals and vision into the culture of your business. Create an atmosphere where your beliefs are reflected and where workers are inspired to match their goals with the company's overarching objectives. Acknowledge and honor actions that further the mission and vision.

Make decisions based on your vision and mission. When faced with critical choices, remember your mission and vision. Consider whether the choice is in line with your values and long-term objectives. This will assist you in making decisions that align with your mission and overall vision.

Always assess and improve: As your company grows, make sure your vision and purpose are still pertinent and in line with your objectives by periodically reviewing them. Get input from interested parties and change as necessary. A dynamic vision and mission statement will help your company stay on course and flexible in the face of changing conditions.

Establishing your vision and goals paves the way for a purpose-driven company that prioritizes sustained success. Your mission will direct your daily actions, while your vision will inspire and encourage you. Writing a strong business plan can be accomplished with confidence if you have a well-defined goal in mind.

2.2 Setting clear goals and objectives

One of the most important steps in creating a strong business strategy is defining your goals and objectives. Making wise decisions and tracking progress becomes challenging in the absence of a defined goal and direction. This section will discuss the value of defining goals and objectives, how to do it successfully, and how they affect your company's ability to succeed.

2.2.1 The Value of Having Objectives and Goals

Your business's roadmap is provided by your goals and objectives. They act as a beacon of light, assisting you in maintaining motivation and focus while you pursue your entrepreneurial goals. You and your team can develop a sense of direction and purpose by establishing specific goals and objectives. The following are some main justifications for why goal-setting is crucial:

1. Focus and Clarity

Clarifying your goals and where you want your business to go is made easier when you set goals and targets. It gives you a sharp focus and keeps you from becoming sidetracked by unimportant opportunities or chores. You can focus your resources and efforts on reaching your goals when you have a clear direction in mind.

2. Assessment and Measuring

Objectives and goals offer a standard by which to gauge development and assess achievement. You may track your progress and decide if you are on track or need to make modifications by defining clear, quantifiable goals. By regularly reviewing your objectives, you can find areas for development and make well-informed decisions that will advance your company.

3. Accountability and Motivation

You and your team will feel more motivated and purposeful when you have well-defined goals and objectives. A shared vision and a sense of ownership are fostered when everyone knows what they are aiming for. Setting and achieving goals gives people a sense of accountability since they act as benchmarks for assessing both individual and group success.

4. Allocation of Resources

You can more efficiently manage your resources when you have goals and objectives. You may make the most use of your time, money, and other resources by determining your priorities and matching them with your objectives. By doing this, you can be sure that your resources are being used where they will yield the highest return.

2.2.2 Specifying Objectives and Goals

It is crucial to describe goals and objectives in a way that is time-bound, relevant, measurable, and specific (SMART) in order to establish clear goals and objectives. An explanation of each part is provided below:

1. Particular

Objectives and goals must be precise and well-defined. Make specific statements about your goals and stay away from generalizations. Rather than simply stating "increase sales," an explicit objective could be something like "increase sales by 20% in the next quarter."

2. Quantifiable

Measurable goals and objectives will allow you to monitor your progress and assess your level of achievement. Identify the measurements, also known as key performance indicators (KPIs), that will enable you to track your advancement toward the objective. For instance, you can use a customer happiness score or the quantity of favorable customer reviews to gauge your success if your objective is to raise customer contentment.

3. Doable

Realistic and reachable goals and objectives are essential. Setting lofty objectives is vital, but they should also be doable. When you set goals, take into account your strengths, available resources, and limitations. Unrealistic goals can cause dissatisfaction and demotivation.

4. Applicable

Your goals and objectives should be in line with your company's overarching vision and mission. They should support the expansion and prosperity of your company and be in line with your long-term goals. Make sure your objectives have a clear impact on the strategic direction of your company.

5. Time-limited

There should be a deadline or set period of time for goals and objectives. This keeps you focused and gives you a sense of urgency. Establish attainable deadlines that will let you monitor your progress and make the required corrections as you go.

2.2.3 Matching Your Vision with Your Goals and Objectives

Your entire corporate vision and mission should be in line with your goals and objectives. They ought to represent your company's ideals and long-term goals. Think about the following while establishing goals:

1. Extended Vision

Establish your company's long-term goals first. What goals do you have for the upcoming five, ten, or twenty years? Achieving this vision should be the first step towards achieving your goals and objectives.

2. The Mission Proclamation

The goals and core principles of your company are stated in your mission statement. It functions as a compass for making decisions. Make sure your aims and objectives support the fulfillment of your mission statement and are in line with it.

3. Fundamental Principles

Decide which fundamental values best describe your company. Your organization's culture should be reflected in your goals and objectives, which should be in line with these principles.

4. The SWOT evaluation

Analyze your company's strengths, weaknesses, opportunities, and threats (SWOT) to find internal and external variables that could have an impact. Make goals based on this analysis that will help you take advantage of opportunities, strengthen your areas of weakness, and reduce dangers.

Your vision, purpose, values, and SWOT analysis should all be in line with your goals and objectives to make sure that every move you take advances the general prosperity of your company.

2.2.4 Sharing and Tracking Objectives and Goals

It's critical to properly convey your goals and objectives to your team after you've defined them. Make sure that everyone is aware of each goal's relevance, purpose, and anticipated results. As a result, there is a sense of accountability and common knowledge.

Keep a close eye on the advancement of your goals and objectives. Make use of key performance indicators (KPIs) to gauge your advancement.

Celebrate your progress and acknowledge your accomplishments along the way. Make modifications as needed. Everyone remains motivated and focused on reaching the intended results when goals and objectives are regularly communicated and tracked.

To sum up, defining precise goals and objectives is an essential first step in writing a strong business plan. They give direction, clarity, and concentration and act as a yardstick for tracking development and gauging achievement. You may design a plan for the expansion and development of your company by setting clear, quantifiable, realistic, relevant, and time-bound goals and coordinating them with your vision, mission, and core values. To make sure that everyone is in agreement and working toward the same goal, regular goal monitoring and communication are essential.

2.3 Examining the Market Environment

Developing a successful firm requires a thorough awareness of the competitive environment in which you want to operate. You may identify your competitors, evaluate their advantages and disadvantages, and figure out how to set yourself apart from the competition and obtain a competitive edge by doing a competitive landscape analysis. This section will walk you through the process of examining the competitive environment and give you the resources and know-how to help you make wise decisions for your company.

2.3.1 Recognizing Your Rivals

Finding your direct and indirect competitors is the first step in studying the competitive environment. Businesses that cater to the same target market as yours and offer comparable goods or services are considered direct rivals. Conversely, indirect competitors can provide distinct goods or services, but they would still fight for the same clients. You can begin by performing market research, looking through industry data, and examining consumer feedback to determine who your competitors are. You can also look for companies in your area or industry using online resources and platforms.

After you've determined who your rivals are, it's critical to learn more about them. This entails being aware of their clientele, pricing schemes, marketing approaches, and company methods. You may find out what is successful in the market and how to set your company apart from the competition by researching your rivals.

2.3.2 Evaluating the Advantages and Disadvantages of Rivals

The next stage is to evaluate your competitors' strengths and shortcomings after you've identified them. This study will assist you in identifying the unique selling points of your rivals as well as potential weak points. When evaluating the advantages and disadvantages of competitors, some things to take into account are:

Product or service quality: Assess the level of quality provided by your rivals and contrast it with your own. Seek out opportunities to stand out from the competition and offer better goods or services.

Pricing: Examine the pricing tactics of your rivals to see whether you can provide a more value-for-money product or if they are competitive.

Reputation of brand: Evaluate the standing and perception of your rivals' brands. Think about how their messaging and brand positioning appeal to consumers and how you might position your own brand to stand out.

Marketing and sales strategy: Research the strategies used by your rivals in these areas. Seek out novel ideas or weaknesses in their plans that you may take advantage of to have an edge over them.

Customer experience: Look at the general manner in which your rivals deal with their clients and the services they offer. Determine where you can provide a better experience and forge closer bonds with your clients.

You may find ways to set your company apart from the competition and create plans to beat them in the market by carefully examining the advantages and disadvantages of each.

2.3.3 Making Your Company Stand Out

It's time to create a plan to set your company apart from the competition once you have a firm grasp on their advantages and disadvantages. To stand out in a crowded market and draw clients, differentiation is essential. Here are some tactics to think about:

Unique value proposition: Determine what sets your company apart and make sure your target audience knows. This could be a special feature of your offering, an alternative payment plan, or first-rate customer support.

Innovation: To stay ahead of the competition, always develop and enhance your goods and services. This could be utilizing technology, releasing new features, or coming up with original ways to address problems that customers are having.

Customer experience: Put your best foot forward to offer outstanding service at all points of contact. This entails tailored exchanges, timely customer assistance, and a smooth checkout procedure.

Branding and messaging: Create a distinctive brand identity that appeals to your intended audience. Create persuasive messaging that explains the value your company provides and helps you stand out from the competition.

Targeting certain niches within your target market and customizing your goods and services to fit their particular requirements is known as niche targeting. You can establish yourself as an authority in a particular field and attract clients who are searching for specialized services by concentrating on that specialization.

You can get a competitive edge that will draw clients and make you stand out in the market by differentiating your firm.

2.3.4 Keeping an eye on and adjusting to the market environment
Examining the competitive environment is a continuous process. It's critical to keep an eye on your rivals and modify your tactics as necessary. Keep a watch out for emerging markets, shifts in consumer tastes, and industry developments. To make sure you stay ahead of the competition, examine and update your competitive analysis on a regular basis.

Additionally, ask for and act upon consumer feedback to enhance your offerings in terms of goods and services as well as the general customer experience. Maintaining flexibility and adaptability to market developments can help you set up your company for long-term success.

To sum up, one of the most important steps in creating a successful firm is studying the competitive environment. You can obtain a competitive edge and draw clients by recognizing your rivals, evaluating their advantages and disadvantages, and setting yourself apart from the competition. To stay ahead of the competition, keep an eye on the competitive environment and adjust your plans as necessary. You can position your company for development and success and make well-informed decisions if you have a complete awareness of the competitive landscape.

2.4 Formulating a Plan of Action

It is now time to create a strategic plan for your company once you have clarified your goals, assessed the competitive environment, and established your vision. A strategic roadmap is a high-level plan that lists the major tasks and completion dates necessary to accomplish your long-term goals. It acts as a roadmap to support you in maintaining concentration, making wise choices, and allocating resources wisely.

2.4.1 Clarifying Your Strategic Goals

It's critical to specify your strategic objectives precisely before you can create a strategic plan. These goals should provide your company with a clear direction and be consistent with your overarching vision and mission. Strategic objectives are overarching goals that specify your long-term aims. They ought to be SMART goals—specific, measurable, realistic, pertinent, and time-bound.

If you are introducing a software-as-a-service (SaaS) platform, for instance, your strategic goals could be:

In the next two years, increase market share by twenty percent.
Take your business global in the following three years.
Within the next year, reach a 90% client retention rate.
Your strategy roadmap will be built upon the smaller, more manageable goals and actions that you may achieve by first identifying your strategic objectives.

2.4.2 Determining Important Projects and Benchmarks

After defining your strategic goals, the next step is to choose the major projects and benchmarks that will enable you to reach those goals. Milestones are the precise times at which you expect to achieve particular results, whereas initiatives are the large projects or actions that must be carried out to reach your goals.

Think about the following while identifying important initiatives:

Which large-scale initiatives or tasks must be finished in order to meet your strategic goals?
Which resources—financial, human, or technological—will be needed for each initiative?

What is each initiative's projected timeline?

For instance, if one of your strategic goals is to gain 20% more market share in the following two years, some important projects could be:

starting a focused marketing push to draw in new clients.

increasing consumer pleasure by improving the product's user experience.

enlarging your sales force to target new clients and markets.

After determining which projects are most important, you can divide them into more manageable tasks and give each one a deadline as well as a set of duties.

2.4.3 Setting Initiatives and Resource Priorities

Since not all projects are equal, it's critical to rank them in order of their impact and viability. Setting priorities for your projects will help you focus on the most crucial and attainable objectives while also ensuring that you are allocating your resources in an efficient manner.

As you rank initiatives, take into account the following:

What possible effects might each endeavor have on your strategic goals?

How feasible is each endeavor in terms of time, money, and experience?

Regarding your overall timeline, how urgent is each initiative?

You can focus on the most important aspects of your business and make well-informed decisions about where to devote your resources by setting priorities for your efforts.

2.4.4 Formulating a Pictorial Roadmap

The most effective strategic roadmaps are clear and visually appealing. You may clearly and succinctly explain your strategy plan to investors, team members, and stakeholders by creating a visual roadmap.

To construct a visual roadmap, you can use a variety of tools and methods, including:

Gantt charts: These are bar charts that show your efforts' and milestones' timelines visually. They offer a concise synopsis of the dependencies and project timeline.

Kanban boards: On a kanban board, tasks are represented by cards or sticky notes, and completion phases are shown by columns. They offer a graphic depiction of your projects' advancement.

Mind maps are graphic diagrams that assist with concept organization and connection. You can use them to chart the connections between your strategic goals, projects, and benchmarks.

To make sure that everyone is on the same page and working toward the same objectives, select the visualization style that best suits you and your team. You should also communicate and update your roadmap on a frequent basis.

2.4.5 Examining and Modifying Your Schedule

A strategic plan should be periodically reviewed and modified to account for shifts in internal capabilities, external market conditions, and the business environment. Maintaining an agile and responsive approach to new possibilities and challenges can be achieved by periodically evaluating and modifying your roadmap.

As you go over your roadmap, keep the following in mind:

Do your current activities and milestones still support your strategic goals?

Has the competitive landscape or the market changed in a way that calls for modifications to your roadmap?

Exist any fresh prospects or difficulties that require attention?

Make any necessary revisions to your roadmap in light of your evaluation, and let your team and stakeholders know about them. You can make sure that your company stays on course and moves closer to its long-term goals by routinely reviewing and modifying your plan.

To sum up, creating a strategic roadmap is an essential first step in growing your company from the ground up to launch. You can successfully navigate the difficulties and uncertainties of the entrepreneurial journey and improve your chances of success by defining your strategic objectives, identifying important initiatives and milestones, prioritizing initiatives, creating a visual roadmap, and routinely reviewing and adjusting your roadmap.

SECURING FUNDING FOR YOUR VENTURE

3.1 Recognizing Various Financing Choices

One of the most important steps in making your business idea a reality is obtaining money. It can be difficult to realize your goal and get through the early phases of your business without enough funding. This section will examine the different funding sources accessible to business owners and offer advice on selecting the best funding plan for their venture.

3.1.1 Self-starting

One type of fundraising called "bootstrapping" entails financing your company with your own funds or assets. With this strategy, you can avoid taking on debt or giving up equity while still having total control over your business. Although some entrepreneurs may find bootstrapping to be a feasible alternative, it does necessitate careful financial planning and the capacity to properly manage minimal resources.

One benefit of bootstrapping is that it lets you keep total control and authority over your company's decisions. You may concentrate on laying a strong foundation for your business since you are free to make decisions without interference from outside parties. Bootstrapping, however, could make it more difficult for you to grow quickly because you might not have enough money to invest in prospects for expansion.

3.1.2 Family and Friends

Asking friends and relatives for financial help is another popular way for businesses to raise capital. This strategy entails reaching out to people in your personal network and making a business presentation to those who have faith in and confidence in you. Obtaining cash from friends and family can be a great way to get started, especially if your business is just getting started.

You should always handle requests for funding from friends and relatives in a professional manner. Handle it like a formal business transaction, outlining the conditions and goals of the investment in detail. To prevent any potential pressure on personal connections, it is imperative to maintain open and honest communication.

3.1.3 Syndicated Capitalists

Angel investors are those that lend money to firms in their early stages in return for convertible debt or stock. Usually, these financiers are wealthy people or seasoned business owners seeking to fund potential projects. Angel investors frequently offer important industry connections and mentorship in addition to cash.

A strong business strategy and an eye-catching pitch deck are essential when pursuing angel investors. Your value offer, market opportunity, and growth potential must all be clearly expressed. Be ready to show why your business is worth investing in. Angel investors are searching for businesses with great teams and tremendous growth potential.

3.1.4 Investment Funding

Investment businesses known as venture capital (VC) firms fund entrepreneurs in return for stock. Usually investing in fast-growing sectors, these organizations seek out businesses that have the capacity to yield substantial returns on their capital. Startups can get the financial resources they require from venture capital funding to grow quickly and enter new industries.

It can be very competitive to get venture capital funding. Venture capital firms screen through a large number of investment ideas to identify the most promising ones. Demonstrating a viable business model, a promising market potential, and a competent management team are necessary to draw in venture funding. It is critical to conduct in-depth research on VC firms that are compatible with your sector and growth stage.

3.1.5 Internet fundraising

In recent years, crowdfunding has become more and more popular as a means for business owners to raise capital from a huge number of people. Using a crowdfunding platform, a campaign is created, and awards or equity are offered in return for monetary donations. Through crowdfunding, business owners may simultaneously collect money, get early customer interest in their idea, and validate it.

Various forms of crowdsourcing exist, such as donation-based crowdfunding, equity crowdfunding, and reward-based crowdfunding. Before starting a crowdfunding campaign, it is important to be aware of the needs and restrictions, as each type has its own set of rules and regulations.

3.1.6 Government Programs and Grants

Entrepreneurs can receive non-repayable funding to boost their company endeavors through grants and government initiatives. These kinds of financing are frequently offered to particular industries, R&D initiatives, or social companies. Government grants and programs can be a great way to get money because they don't need to be repaid or equity given up.

In order to be eligible for grants and government programs, you must fully investigate your alternatives and comprehend the requirements. It's important to have a strong proposal that explains how your company fits with the program's goals because the application process can be competitive.

3.1.7 Finance for Debt

Debt financing is taking out loans from lenders or financial organizations and paying them back over a certain time period with interest. This kind of financing can give business owners the money they need to launch or expand their enterprises. There are other ways to finance debt, such as bank loans, credit lines, or microloans.

It is critical to evaluate your ability to repay the borrowed funds when thinking about debt financing. The terms and conditions, including interest rates, repayment plans, and any collateral requirements, must be fully understood by you. Working with an accountant or financial expert can help you determine whether debt financing is the right choice for your company.

3.1.8 Incubators and Accelerators

Programs known as incubators and accelerators give new businesses tools, finance, and guidance to help them expand more quickly. Usually, these programs include workspace, financial investment, and networking opportunities with seasoned business owners and professionals in the field. Incubators and accelerators can be a great choice for early-stage companies trying to establish themselves and improve their business plans.

You must go through a competitive application procedure in order to get accepted into an accelerator or incubator program. It is essential to investigate and select programs that correspond with your industry and growth stage, as these programs frequently have particular requirements and focus areas.

In summary
Gaining knowledge of the various funding sources accessible to business owners is crucial to obtaining the funds required to start and expand your enterprise. Before choosing a funding option, it is important to assess your unique needs and goals, as each one has pros and cons of its own. You may improve your chances of obtaining the capital required to transform your business idea into a profitable endeavor by carefully weighing your funding possibilities and creating a strong funding strategy.

3.2 Crafting an Effective Pitch Deck

An essential tool for any entrepreneur looking to raise money for their business is a pitch deck. It is a succinct and eye-catching presentation that summarizes the salient features of your company and emphasizes its growth prospects. We will go over the key components of an effective pitch deck in this section and provide you with useful advice on how to make a strong and convincing presentation.

3.2.1 Creating a Captivating Start

Your pitch deck's opening establishes the mood for the whole thing. Potential investors should be drawn to it and motivated to find out more about your company. The following are essential components for your introduction:

Elevator Pitch: Introduce your company and its distinct value proposition with a succinct and engaging elevator pitch. Focus on the problem you are solving and the market opportunity, and keep it succinct and powerful.

Mission and Vision: To show your long-term objectives and aspirations, clearly define your mission and vision statements. This will make your company's goals and direction more clear to potential investors.

Founder Story: Give a succinct and interesting account of your background and entrepreneurial path. Emphasize your enthusiasm, knowledge, and any pertinent accomplishments that show you can carry out your business plan successfully.

3.2.2 Outlining the Issue and Its Resolution

Businesses that meet market demands and find solutions to actual challenges attract investors. You must describe the issue your target audience is facing in detail in this area and offer your creative solution. The following is an excellent way to communicate the issue and its resolution:

Market Analysis: Give a succinct synopsis of the market you are aiming for, outlining its size, potential for expansion, and major trends. Utilize reliable data and statistics to back up your assertions and illustrate the size of the industry.

Problem Statement: Clearly state the issue that

your intended audience is having. To make it relatable and interesting, provide tales or examples from real life. Demonstrate that you are well aware of the difficulties and problems that your potential clients are facing.

Solution: Outline your approach and describe how it successfully solves the stated issue. Emphasize the special qualities and advantages of your good or service and give reasons why it is better than the competition. Prototypes or product demos can be used to provide a tangible and understandable answer.

3.2.3 Presenting Competitive Advantage and Market Potential

Investors are looking for proof of market potential as well as a distinct competitive edge that makes your company stand out from the competition. You must prove in this part that your company has a solid market position and the capacity for long-term growth. The following are some excellent ways to illustrate your competitive advantage and market potential:

Target Market: Clearly state who your target market is and share information about its psychographics, purchasing patterns, and demographics. Demonstrate your thorough comprehension of your clients' requirements.

Market Validation: Provide any data from consumer surveys or market research that demonstrates that there is a need for your good or service. Provide evidence of market traction through case studies, early adopter success stories, or testimonials.

Competitive Analysis: Clearly state your competitive advantage by doing a detailed study of your rivals. Emphasize the distinctive qualities, intellectual property, strategic alliances, or innovative business plan that make your company stand out.

3.2.4 Presenting the Financial Projections and Business Model

Investors are interested in learning how your company makes money and intends to turn a profit. You must describe your business plan and include accurate financial estimates in this part. Here's how to properly present your financial projections and business model:

Business Model: Clearly state how your company makes money, including how it does so through sales of products, subscription services, advertising, and other sources. Explain your customer acquisition strategy, distribution methods, and pricing approach.

Financial Projections: Provide accurate financial estimates that account for anticipated revenue, costs, and profitability. To help readers grasp the facts, provide tables, graphs, and charts. Be open and honest about your assumptions, and give a precise schedule for reaching important benchmarks.

Key Metrics: Determine and emphasize the key metrics that are essential to the success of your company. This might include the attrition rate, client acquisition cost, customer lifetime value, or any other pertinent data that shows your company's potential for development and financial stability.

3.2.5 Highlighting the Group and Achievements

Investors support the team behind ideas in addition to the ideas themselves. You must highlight your team's qualifications, experience, and performance history in this section. Emphasize the significant accomplishments you have made as well as the goals you have for the future. Here's how to successfully highlight your group's accomplishments:

Team Introduction: Give a brief overview of your main team members' backgrounds and areas of expertise. Emphasize any prior industry recognition, awards, or special skills that make your team a strong fit to carry out the business plan.

Partners and consultants: List any illustrious alliances or strategic consultants that enhance the legitimacy and worth of your company. Mentors, industry experts, and alliances with well-established businesses could all fall into this category.

Milestones: List the significant accomplishments you have made thus far, such as revenue, customer acquisition, or product development milestones. Describe the future benchmarks you hope to hit and the approximate time it will take you to get there.

3.2.6 Creating an Eye-Catchy and Harmonious Presentation

Investor attention is largely attracted to and retained by the visual appearance of your presentation deck. The following advice can help you create a coherent and aesthetically pleasing presentation:

Consistent Branding: Throughout your presentation, use recognizable branding components, including typefaces, colors, and logos. This results in a polished and unified appearance.

Visuals and Graphics: To make complex information easier to understand and visually appealing, include visuals like charts, graphs, photos, and infographics. Steer clear of clutter, and make sure your images help readers understand what you've written.

Text that is Easy to Read and Clear: Make sure your writing is easy to read and clear. To break up the content and make it easier to browse, use headings, bullet points, and brief sentences.

Engaging Layout: Create a gripping narrative and direct the viewer's attention with an engaging layout for your slides. Slide transitions and animations should be used sparingly to prevent audience distraction.

Keep in mind that a pitch deck is meant to supplement your oral presentation, so concentrate on telling a gripping story and keep the material brief. Make sure you can confidently and effectively convey your business idea and its prospects for success by practicing your pitch often.

3.3 Making Your Idea Known to Investors

The next important stage is to get money for your firm after you have a strong business plan and a clear vision. Even though there are many different fundraising methods accessible, seeking investors is one of the most popular and efficient ways to raise funds. However, if you are new to the world of entrepreneurship, seeking investors and pitching your idea might be a difficult undertaking. This section will walk you through the process of approaching potential investors and creating an engaging pitch that will grab their interest and persuade them to put money into your venture.

3.3.1 Selecting the Appropriate Investors

Finding the ideal investors for your company is crucial before you begin pursuing them. It's important to do your homework and locate investors who have a history of funding companies that are comparable to yours because not all investors will be interested in your sector or stage of development. Seek out investors who recognize the potential in your project and who genuinely care about your sector. By doing this, you'll have a better chance of attracting investors who can offer helpful advice and support in addition to their willingness to contribute.

3.3.2 Developing a Powerful Pitch Deck

A pitch deck is a succinct presentation that gives a synopsis of your company and emphasizes its distinct selling point. It is a crucial tool for drawing in investors and showcasing the possibilities of your concept. Remember that investors receive a lot of pitches every day, so it's important to make yours stand out when creating your pitch deck. The following are essential components for your pitch deck:

Problem Statement: Clearly state the issue that

your company is trying to resolve. Describe the problem's importance and how your approach solves it.

Solution: Outline how your approach addresses the issue better than the options now available. Emphasize the special qualities and advantages of your goods or services.

Market Opportunity: Showcase the size and room for expansion of your intended audience. To bolster your arguments and demonstrate the significant market need for your solution, use data and figures.

Business Model: Describe how you plan to make money and turn a profit for your company. Describe your pricing plan, your methods of distribution, and any other pertinent information regarding your company concept.

Competitive Advantage: Emphasize what makes your company unique from rivals. This could be any element that offers you a competitive advantage in the market, such as proprietary technology, a potent brand, or exclusive alliances.

Team: Give a brief overview of the experience, knowledge, and skills of your team members. Investors are interested in learning that you have a committed and competent staff that can carry out your business plan successfully.

Financial Projections: Give investors an idea of the

possible return on their investment by providing reasonable financial projections. Provide essential financial indicators, spending breakdowns, and revenue projections.

3.3.3 Establishing Connections and Networking
Reaching out to investors is about more than just selling your idea; it's also about networking and establishing relationships. Attend conferences, networking events, and industry events to meet investors and build relationships. It takes time to establish connections with investors, so be persistent and patient. Have deep discussions with them, pay attention to their opinions, and genuinely express interest in their knowledge and perspectives. Establishing a robust network of investors can aid in obtaining capital and offer invaluable coaching and direction during your startup path.

3.3.4 Making an Eye-Catching Proposal
Being well-prepared is essential when presenting your proposal to potential investors. Repeatedly practice your pitch until you feel at ease and secure in its delivery. The following advice will assist you in making a strong pitch:

Be Brief: Make sure your pitch is brief and direct. Because investors are pressed for time, make every word matter. Keep your attention on what matters most to your company, and don't get bogged down in technicalities.

Tell a Story: Construct an engaging story that encapsulates your company's core values. Employ narrative strategies to emotionally connect investors and create a lasting impression in their minds.

Show Your Passion and Confidence: Potential investors want to know that you have a strong sense of passion for your concept and confidence in its viability. When making your case, be passionate and forceful.

Address Any Potential Concerns: Be aware of and prepare for any possible objections or worries from investors. Be ready to respond to inquiries regarding potential hazards, scalability, and market competitiveness.

Showcase Traction: In your pitch, emphasize any accomplishments you have made thus far, such as early client acquisitions or milestones reached. Gaining traction can dramatically boost your company's perceived worth and trustworthiness.

3.3.5 Checking in and Establishing Credibility
It's critical to stay in touch and follow up with investors once you present your idea. To thank them for their time and thoughtfulness, send them a thank-you email or note. Inform them of your accomplishments and growth. It's important to establish credibility and trust with investors, so communicate openly and truthfully. Keeping a good rapport can lead to future opportunities or

recommendations to other investors, even if the investor chooses not to invest at this time.

Recall that pitching your idea to investors and reaching out to them is a skill that can be developed with experience and practice. Be receptive to criticism, take lessons from every pitch, and keep improving. You can find the proper investors who will back your idea from conception to launch if you are persistent and have a strong pitch.

3.4 Reaching and Sealing Financing Agreements
One of the most important steps in making your business idea a reality is securing money. This chapter will examine the craft of negotiating and concluding funding agreements, giving you the information and abilities you need to obtain the capital required to establish and expand your company.

3.4.1 Comprehending the Finance Environment

It's critical to comprehend the financial environment and the range of possibilities accessible to entrepreneurs before beginning the negotiation process. A multitude of sources, such as government grants, crowdsourcing websites, angel investors, and venture capitalists, can provide money. Finding the best funding source for your company requires careful consideration since each one has different conditions, expectations, and criteria.

Professional investors known as venture capitalists (VCs) lend money to high-potential firms in exchange for stock. Usually, they make investments in startups that have the potential to grow quickly and yield large profits. Venture capitalists (VCs) frequently contribute not only capital but also industry knowledge and important relationships.

Individuals that invest their personal money in startups in exchange for stock are known as angel investors. They can offer cash as well as invaluable mentorship and direction, as they are frequently accomplished entrepreneurs themselves. Compared to regular venture capitalists, angel investors are more prepared to take chances and typically invest in early-stage enterprises.

In recent years, crowdfunding platforms have become more and more popular as a means for business owners to acquire capital from a large number of people, frequently in exchange for incentives like product pre-orders. By utilizing this approach, entrepreneurs can validate their concept and get early traction while connecting with a larger pool of possible supporters and clients.

Another possible source of income is grants and subsidies from the government, especially for companies operating in specialized areas or industries. These awards are frequently intended to encourage innovation, R&D, or the creation of jobs. Even though applying for government grants can be more difficult and time-consuming, if successful, they can significantly improve your company.

3.4.2 Getting Ready for the Bargain

Being organized is essential before engaging in negotiations with possible investors. Understanding your company's financial requirements, appraising them, and creating an engaging proposal that emphasizes your venture's distinctive value proposition and development prospects are all part of this preparation.

To begin, figure out how much money you'll need to accomplish your company's objectives. Examine your financial estimates carefully, accounting for things like working capital needs, marketing expenditures, product development costs, and operations costs. You can use this analysis to calculate how much money you need to raise and how much equity you are willing to give up in exchange.

Next, it's critical to appropriately value your business. The process of valuation is intricate and involves several considerations, such as the competitive environment, revenue forecasts, market potential, and intellectual property. To arrive at a reasonable and realistic valuation, think about reviewing industry benchmarks or getting expert financial guidance.

Another important part of being ready for negotiations is creating an engaging pitch deck. Your business idea, market opportunity, competitive advantage, and growth strategy should all be clearly communicated in your pitch deck. Financial estimates, significant achievements, and the possible return on investment for possible investors should also be included. Having a visually striking and well-designed pitch deck can help you stand out from the competition and make a big impression.

3.4.3 The Craft of Bargaining

Achieving a mutually beneficial connection with potential investors while defending your company's best interests during funding negotiations is a delicate balance to be struck. The following are some essential ideas to bear in mind when negotiating:

Recognize your value: Recognize the worth of your

company and the distinctive offering it makes to the market. Have faith in your ability to communicate the growth potential and ROI that your company provides.

Establish definite goals: Establish your goals for the negotiation and rank them. Determine which terms and conditions are indisputable to you, and be ready to make concessions on the rest. Knowing exactly what you want out of the discussion can help you maintain focus.

Investigate your investors: Do extensive research on possible investors before initiating any negotiations. Recognize their areas of competence, prior investments, and investing criteria. With this information, you'll be able to adjust your pitch and negotiating approach to suit their needs and goals.

Develop relationships: Long-term relationships can be built during negotiations, which are about more than just business deals. Spend some time learning about the investor's objectives, worries, and driving forces. Be genuinely interested in their knowledge and solicit their counsel. Developing a good relationship can help you get better terms and continued assistance after the initial funding.

Be adaptable. Giving and taking are common in negotiations. Be willing to make concessions and look for original solutions that satisfy the requirements of both sides. Recall that the objective is to arrive at a win-win solution that lays the groundwork for a fruitful collaboration.

Seek legal assistance: In order to evaluate and negotiate the conditions of the funding agreement, it is imperative that legal counsel be involved as the negotiations move forward. A lawyer with knowledge of startup capital can assist in making sure the contract safeguards your rights and is in line with your company's goals.

3.4.4 Sealing the Offer

It is now time to finalize the financial agreement after negotiations have produced a positive result. Finalizing the terms and conditions, signing the required legal paperwork, and transferring the money are all part of closing the sale. The following are some essential actions to take when closing:

Create and evaluate legal documents: Create the required legal agreements, including the shareholder agreement, investment agreement, and term sheet, in collaboration with your legal advisor. The parameters of the investment are described in these documents, together with the funding amount, equity ownership, investor rights, and any other terms or limitations.

Perform due diligence: Investors may carry out due diligence before closing the deal in order to confirm the veracity of the information supplied and evaluate any possible hazards. Be ready to respond to any queries or concerns expressed throughout this process, as well as to provide more supporting documentation.

Seek professional help: During the closing process, it is imperative that you consult your legal counsel and financial consultants for professional advice. They can help you navigate the deal's financial and legal ramifications and make sure that all appropriate precautions are taken to safeguard your interests.

Sign the agreement. The investment agreement and any other pertinent documents should be signed once all parties have agreed to the terms and conditions. This formalizes the agreements and prepares the groundwork for the subsequent stage of your business venture.

Careful planning, skillful negotiating, and a deep awareness of the financial landscape are necessary for closing funding arrangements. You will be well-equipped to handle the negotiating process and obtain the capital required to realize your business idea if you adhere to the guidelines provided in this chapter. Recall that discussions offer a chance to forge connections and establish the groundwork for long-term success in addition to the monetary exchange.

BUILDING A STRONG TEAM

4.1 Determining Important Positions and Duties

Determining the important tasks and duties

inside your company is essential to developing a robust and prosperous enterprise. Every team member is essential to the overall success of your project, and knowing your roles will help you establish a productive and harmonious work environment. This section will discuss the significance of defining important roles and duties as well as offer suggestions for managing and assigning them.

4.1.1 Outlining Important Duties

Clearly defining the various jobs and duties within your business is the first step towards identifying essential roles and responsibilities. Start by evaluating the unique requirements of your company and the everyday chores that must be completed. Think about the various departments that make up your company, including marketing, sales, operations, finance, and customer support.

For instance, a business may require a CEO or founder to provide overall strategic direction and leadership, a CFO to oversee financial matters, a CMO to supervise marketing and branding initiatives, and a head of operations to guarantee seamless daily operations. Depending on the type of your company, you might also need to designate positions like product managers, customer support representatives, and sales representatives.

4.1.2 Evaluating Competencies and Knowledge

After defining the major responsibilities inside your company, it's critical to evaluate the knowledge and abilities needed for each role. Take into account the particular training, background, and expertise required to carry out the duties entailed in each post.

Spend some time assessing the advantages and disadvantages of your current team members and possible new recruitment. Seek out people who have the expertise and experience required to carry out the duties of each post. It's crucial to take into account the possibility of team growth and development since you might need to offer mentorship or training to help members improve the abilities required for their positions.

4.1.3 Delegating Accountabilities

Assigning tasks to each team member comes after you have determined the important roles and evaluated the knowledge and abilities needed. Clearly outline each role's responsibilities and goals, then successfully convey them to your team.

When delegating tasks, take into account each person's interests and strengths. Finding the perfect candidate for a position can have a significant positive impact on output and job satisfaction. To prevent confusion or overlap, make sure that the delegation of responsibility is transparent and clear.

4.1.4 Creating a Collaborative Setting

Assigning roles and tasks is just one aspect of creating a great team. In order for team members to effectively communicate and cooperate to achieve shared objectives, a collaborative work atmosphere must be fostered. Provide chances for cooperation and idea sharing, and promote direct and honest communication.

Encourage a respectful and trusting atmosphere inside your company. Members of the team should be urged to assist and support one another, as well as acknowledge and honor individual and group accomplishments. Establishing a collaborative atmosphere allows you to leverage the combined abilities and knowledge of your group, resulting in heightened creativity and efficiency.

4.1.5 Assessing and Modifying Positions
It's critical to periodically assess the efficacy of the roles and responsibilities inside your organization as it develops and expands. Determine whether the allocated responsibilities still meet the evolving demands of your company and adapt as needed.

Evaluate each team member's performance on a regular basis and offer helpful criticism to enable them to develop. Be willing to redefine responsibilities as well as create new ones in order to adapt to the evolving needs of your company. Building a solid and resilient team requires a high degree of adaptability and flexibility.

In summary
One of the most important steps in creating

a solid and prosperous company is identifying the important jobs and duties. You may build a high-performing team that propels the expansion and success of your business by clearly defining positions, evaluating candidates' abilities and experience, assigning duties, encouraging teamwork, and routinely reviewing and modifying roles. Recall that creating a good team is a continual process that calls for constant attention and effort.

4.2 Seeking and Selecting Elite Personnel

Developing a solid team is essential to any company's success. As an entrepreneur, you must surround yourself with gifted people who can support the expansion of your company by sharing your vision and lending their knowledge and experience. We will look at the process of finding and employing great talent for your business in this part.

4.2.1 Clarifying Your Needs for Hiring

It is crucial to specify the jobs and tasks you need to fill inside your organization before you start the hiring process. Determine the credentials and experience level you are searching for by first evaluating the abilities and knowledge needed for each role. This will assist you in crafting precise job descriptions and drawing in applicants who meet the requirements.

Take prospective applicants' cultural fit into account as well. In addition to possessing the necessary abilities, your staff should share the same values and work ethics as your business. A peaceful and effective work environment can be ensured by taking cultural fit into consideration during the hiring process.

4.2.2 Creating a Job Description That Works

To draw in eligible applicants, a job description that is well-written is crucial. It should give a concise description of the role, outlining the duties, requirements, and any special criteria. In your job description, be clear and succinct while emphasizing the essential knowledge and expertise you are looking for.

Think about incorporating details on the culture, mission, and values of your company in addition to the technical needs. Candidates will be better able to comprehend and assess their compatibility with the ethos of your company, thanks to this.

4.2.3 Finding applicants

You can source possible candidates for your available roles in a number of ways. Here are some successful tactics:

Internal Referrals: Motivate your current staff members to recommend deserving applicants from their contacts. By providing rewards for successful referrals, you may encourage your staff to get involved in the recruiting process.

Post job openings on well-known job boards and professional networking websites through online job boards. You can access a wider pool of talent by using these platforms, which draw in a diverse group of applicants.

Social media: Use Twitter, Facebook, LinkedIn, and other social media sites to advertise employment opportunities. Participate in pertinent communities and trade associations to raise awareness and draw in prospective applicants.

Professional Networks: Make connections with other experts in your field by going to conferences, industry events, and networking gatherings. Developing contacts with professionals in the field might help you access a talent pool of people who might be interested in working for your company.

4.2.4 Candidate screening and interviews
After receiving resumes and applications, it's time to interview and assess possible applicants. Make a selection of the most qualified applicants for additional assessment by first looking over their credentials and experience.

To evaluate candidates' communication abilities, cultural fit, and overall fitness for the position, conduct preliminary phone or video interviews. Create a list of standard questions to ask each applicant so you can compare their answers in an unbiased manner.

Organize in-person interviews with individuals who make it past the first round of screening to learn more about their qualifications, backgrounds, and prospective contributions to your company. To ensure a good fit within the team and to obtain alternative perspectives, think about including other team members in the interview process.

4.2.5 Evaluating Competencies and Cultural Fit

It is critical to evaluate each candidate's technical proficiency and cultural fit during the interview process. Work samples, case studies, and practical examinations can all be used to assess technical capabilities. These tests will assist you in figuring out whether the applicants have the abilities needed to succeed in their positions.

Assess cultural fit by posing questions that determine how well they mesh with the goals and culture of your organization. Ask candidates how they would react in situations that resemble the culture of your company. This will enable you to determine whether they'll fit in well with your team and advance the expansion of your business.

4.2.6 Verifying Backgrounds and References

It is crucial to verify the information provided by the candidates and run reference checks before making a final decision. To learn more about a candidate's performance, dependability, and work ethic, get in touch with their former employers or professional references. By taking this stage, you may confirm the candidates' credentials and make sure they have a successful track record.

In order to make sure the applicants are qualified for the job and have a spotless record, you should also think about doing background checks. This is especially crucial for jobs that handle sensitive data or call for a high degree of trust.

4.2.7 Bringing an Offer Up and Getting Started

Once the perfect applicant has been found, make a formal job offer that includes the terms and conditions of the position. Be ready to discuss any issues or respond to any queries the candidate may have. After accepting the offer, carry out the onboarding procedure.

In order to guarantee that new hires transition smoothly, effective onboarding is essential. Assist them in understanding their duties and responsibilities and assimilating into the team by providing them with the required tools, training, and assistance. Provide them with a mentor or friend to help them through the first few days and weeks to help them feel like they belong and to quicken their learning curve.

In summary

One of the most important steps in creating a successful company is finding and employing outstanding talent. By establishing your hiring requirements, creating job descriptions that are effective, strategically finding applicants, and carrying out in-depth assessments, you can put together a high-performing team that will propel your company ahead. To foster a supportive and effective work environment, keep in mind to give equal weight to technical proficiency and cultural fit.

4.3 Fostering a Happy and Effective Work Environment

Establishing a constructive and efficient workplace environment is crucial to the prosperity and expansion of any enterprise. In addition to attracting and keeping elite talent, a great workplace culture also promotes innovation, teamwork, and creativity. This section will cover the essential components of creating a great workplace culture and offer doable tactics for creating a productive atmosphere in your business.

4.3.1 Outlining Your Organization's Mission and Values

Establishing your company's goals and values is one of the first steps towards developing a great work culture. These are the guiding concepts that influence how people behave and make decisions in your company. Your company's values ought to be a reflection of its goals and core principles.

Employees experience a sense of purpose and are more likely to be engaged and motivated when they share these beliefs.

Consider the core ideas and tenets that guide your firm before defining your values. Think about the traits you want your staff to possess and the effect you want your business to have on its clients, staff, and community. After you've determined what your values are, make sure your staff knows what they are and incorporates them into every aspect of your workday.

4.3.2 Promoting Honesty in Communication and Teamwork

Collaborating and communicating freely are essential to developing a positive workplace culture. Transparency and trust are promoted when staff members feel free to voice their opinions, worries, and suggestions. Create avenues for communication, such as suggestion boxes, anonymous feedback sites, or frequent team meetings, to foster open discourse.

Encourage cooperation among staff members by forming cross-functional teams and giving them chances to collaborate on projects. To take full advantage of the variety of viewpoints and areas of expertise inside your company, promote knowledge exchanges and brainstorming sessions. You can stimulate innovation and tap into your team's collective intellect by creating a collaborative atmosphere.

4.3.3 Identifying and Embracing Workers

Fostering a positive work culture requires acknowledging and empowering individuals. Employees are more inclined to take responsibility for their work, make decisions, and contribute to the success of the company when they feel empowered. Give them the chance to advance their careers by offering mentorship, training courses, and difficult projects.

Reward and acknowledge staff members for their accomplishments and contributions. Honor outstanding work, recognize achievements, and foster a culture of gratitude. This can be accomplished through official recognition programs, like employee of the month awards, or more casual means, such as a quick message of gratitude or acknowledgment in front of the group at team meetings. Employee empowerment and recognition lead to an engaged and driven staff.

4.3.4 Enhancing Well-Being and Work-Life Equilibrium

Building a positive work culture requires promoting well-being and work-life balance. Encourage workers to uphold a healthy work-life balance by establishing unambiguous guidelines and, when practical, advocating for flexible work schedules. Offer tools and assistance to promote both physical and mental health, such as fitness center access, wellness programs, and mental health resources.

To avoid burnout and increase productivity, encourage breaks and vacation time. Set an example for your team by putting your own health first and encouraging them to do the same. By encouraging well-being and a work-life balance, you foster an environment where your employees' overall health is valued.

4.3.5 Accepting Inclusion and Diversity

In order to establish a productive and healthy work culture, it is imperative to embrace diversity and inclusion. Different viewpoints, experiences, and ideas are brought to the table by a diverse staff, and this can result in more creative solutions and improved decision-making. Encourage an inclusive work environment by supporting equitable opportunities, appreciating and accepting individual diversity, and giving each employee a sense of community.

Put into practice diversity and inclusion programs, such as employee resource groups, diversity recruitment campaigns, and training on unconscious prejudice. Promote candid conversations regarding diversity and inclusion and establish a secure environment where staff members can freely express their viewpoints and experiences. You can cultivate an environment at work where people value and capitalize on their distinct abilities by embracing diversity and inclusion.

4.3.6 Setting an Example

Your actions as a leader set the standard for the culture of work in your company. Set a good example for your team by acting in accordance with the principles and standards you hold dear. Exhibit honesty, openness, and responsibility in your choices and actions. Keep lines of communication open and honest, and listen to what your staff has to say.

Take the time to get to know your staff members and learn about their goals and requirements. Give your team direction and encouragement while enabling them to take responsibility for their work. Setting a good example for your team members encourages them to pursue greatness and fosters a positive work environment.

4.3.7 Ongoing Enhancement and Input

Fostering a positive workplace culture is a continuous effort that calls for feedback and constant improvement. Evaluate the success of your work culture initiatives on a regular basis and change as necessary. To learn about your employees' experiences and pinpoint areas that need work, ask them for feedback via questionnaires, focus groups, or one-on-one talks.

By offering chances for professional development and feedback, foster an environment where learning and development are ongoing processes. Put in place performance management programs that offer frequent praise and feedback. You may establish an environment where your staff members' needs and goals are met by encouraging a culture of feedback and continual development.

In summary
Establishing a productive and upbeat work culture is essential to growing a successful company. You can create a work culture that draws top talent, spurs innovation, and supports the expansion of your company by defining your company values, encouraging open communication and collaboration, empowering and recognizing employees, encouraging work-life balance and well-being, embracing diversity and inclusion, setting an example, improving continuously, and soliciting feedback. Recall that developing a positive workplace culture takes time and regular effort from both managers and staff.

4.4 Gaining Capabilities for Effective Leadership

Building strong leadership abilities as an entrepreneur is essential to the success of your company. Leading a team is only one aspect of leadership; another is inspiring and encouraging others to work toward a common objective. We'll look at the main ideas and tactics in this section to help you develop into a successful leader who can inspire your group to achieve success.

4.4.1 Recognizing Different Leadership Styles
Different leadership philosophies can be applied based on the circumstances and people involved. Knowing the differences in leadership philosophies will help you modify your strategy to fit your team's requirements as well as the difficulties you encounter. These are a few typical leadership philosophies:

Autocratic Leadership: Under this approach, choices are made by the team leader alone. Although this approach can work well in some circumstances, such as during a crisis, it can also result in a lack of creativity and participation from the workforce.

Democratic Leadership: This approach includes the group in decision-making. It increases team members' motivation and productivity by fostering a sense of empowerment and ownership.

Transformational Leadership: Team members of transformational leaders are inspired and motivated to accomplish above and beyond expectations. They develop a future-focused vision and successfully convey it to their team, inspiring them to pursue excellence.

Servant Leadership: Servant leaders put their team members' needs first and strive to advance both their career and personal growth. They put a lot of effort into fostering great working environments and solid partnerships.

Laissez-faire Leadership: This approach entails offering team members a lot of autonomy and decision-making independence. Although it can encourage innovation and creativity, it needs a group of highly competent and driven people.

4.4.2 Crucial Capabilities for Leadership
You must acquire a few essential abilities in order to lead your team effectively. These abilities will allow you to motivate and mentor them. These are a few crucial abilities for a leader:

Good communication is the cornerstone of effective leadership. Your team needs to hear you communicate your vision, expectations, and goals in a clear and concise manner. Furthermore, it is essential to actively listen in order to comprehend the demands and worries of your team members.

Understanding and controlling your own emotions, as well as those of others, is a component of emotional intelligence. It enables you to establish trusting bonds with your teammates and resolve disputes amicably.

Making Decisions: Every day as a leader, you will have to make a lot of decisions. Gaining the ability to make sound decisions requires obtaining pertinent data, weighing the advantages and disadvantages, and selecting options that support your company's objectives.

Solving Problems: Capable problem solvers make effective leaders. They are able to see problems, examine their underlying causes, and come up with original fixes. Developing an environment where problem-solving is valued within your team will boost creativity and output.

Delegation: Effective leadership requires the delegation of duties and responsibilities. It frees up your time to concentrate on strategic projects while enabling you to take advantage of the abilities and capabilities of your team members.

Motivation: An effective leader is able to uplift and encourage their group. You can foster a happy and productive work atmosphere by finding out what drives your team members, whether it's through rewards, recognition, or growth possibilities.

4.4.3 Strategies for Developing Leadership
Gaining good leadership abilities requires constant work. The following are some tactics to help you become a better leader:

Constant Learning: Keep abreast of the newest developments and top leadership techniques. To increase your understanding and abilities, read books, go to seminars, and take part in leadership development initiatives.

Seek Feedback: Make a conscious effort to get input from mentors, peers, and teammates. You'll be able to pinpoint problem areas and obtain fresh insights about your leadership approach as a result.

Set an example for your team and lead by example. Set an example for the traits and conduct you want from the people in your team. They will be motivated to pursue perfection by seeing you as an example.

Mentorship: Look for mentors who can help you along the way as you progress as a leader. When faced with obstacles, take their advice and learn from their experiences.

Empower Your Team: Assign members the freedom and responsibility to decide for themselves and accept responsibility for their work. This will encourage accountability and a sense of empowerment.

Celebrate Success: Acknowledge and honor your team's accomplishments. They will feel more inspired and driven to keep doing their finest work as a result.

In summary

Gaining strong leadership abilities is crucial to your company's success. You may motivate and direct your team to accomplish your company objectives by comprehending various leadership philosophies, gaining essential leadership abilities, and putting into practice successful leadership development techniques. Recall that being a leader involves more than just managing; it also involves inspiring and enabling others to realize their greatest potential.

MASTERING MARKETING AND SALES

5.1 Establishing Your Goal Market

Identifying your target market is one of the most important phases of creating a profitable company. The particular client base that is most likely to be interested in your product or service is known as your target market. Knowing and identifying your target market can help you focus your marketing efforts and create methods that appeal to your ideal clients. This section will discuss the significance of identifying your target market and provide you with useful techniques for locating and comprehending your target demographic.

5.1.1 The Importance of Clearly Determining Your Target Market

It's critical to define your target market for a number of reasons. First of all, it enables you to concentrate your energies and resources on the clients who are most likely to buy your goods or services. Through comprehension of their requirements, inclinations, and actions, you may develop focused advertising strategies that successfully connect with and include your ideal clients.

Second, identifying your target market enables you to set your company apart from rivals. You may customize your product or service to match the unique needs of your target audience and differentiate yourself from the competition by learning what makes them unique. You may gain a competitive advantage and draw in devoted clients who identify with your brand by making this distinction.

Finally, having a clear understanding of your target market helps you spend your marketing money more wisely. Targeting a wide audience will only waste your efforts; instead, you should concentrate on the demographics most likely to become clients. Higher conversion rates and a better return on investment for your marketing efforts can result from this focused approach.

5.1.2 Determining Your Ideal Customer Base
You must collect pertinent data and carry out in-depth market research before you can define your target market. The following procedures can assist you in determining and comprehending your target audience:

Examine your product or service in step one.
Analyze your offering and determine its special qualities and advantages first. Think about the issue it resolves, the value it provides, and the ways it differs from competing products in the market. You may better grasp the precise wants and desires that your product or service satisfies with the use of this investigation.

Step 2: Do industry research.
To learn more about consumer preferences,

market trends, and the competitive environment, conduct industry research. Find out about the market's size, potential for growth, and important players. Your comprehension of market dynamics will expand as a result of this research, which will also assist you in recognizing possibilities and difficulties.

Step 3: Describe the Demographic Features
Aspects including age, gender, economic bracket, degree of education, and occupation are examples of demographic features. To ascertain which demographic groups are most likely to be interested in what you have to offer, analyze your product or service. If you are a premium skincare product seller, for instance, your target market can be composed of well-to-do people in their 30s to 50s who have more money to spend.

Step 4: Take Psychographic Aspects into Account
The psychological and lifestyle traits of your target audience are the main focus of psychographic variables. Take into account their values, habits, interests, and attitudes. For example, if you sell eco-friendly products, those that value sustainability and the environment can be part of your target market.

Step 5: Perform interviews and surveys.
Consider interviewing and surveying potential customers to gain more detailed information about your target market. Inquire about their inclinations, purchasing patterns, and problems.

You will gain insightful knowledge from this primary research and be able to better grasp your target audience.

Step 6: Examine the clients of competitors
Examine the clientele of your rivals to learn more about their intended audience. Look for trends and parallels in their clientele. You can target underserved or possible holes in the market with the aid of this analysis.

5.1.3 Recognizing Your Ideal Clientele
Understanding your target market's demands, motives, and behaviors in great detail is essential after you've determined who they are. Your marketing tactics will be informed by this knowledge, which will also enable you to craft messages that effectively appeal to your target market. The following are some strategies to help you comprehend your target market better:

Perform market analysis.
To keep abreast of the most recent developments and trends in your target market, keep up your market research. Keep an eye on trade periodicals, visit trade exhibitions, and conduct focus groups and surveys with your target market. This continuous research will assist you in modifying your tactics to satisfy changing client demands.

Make personas for buyers.
Create fictionalized versions of your ideal clients, or buyer personas. These personas must contain

specific pain areas and goals, along with psychographic traits and demographic data. You may better understand your target market and adjust your marketing messaging by developing thorough buyer personas.

Examine client information.
Utilize customer data to learn more about the habits and preferences of your target market. Track website traffic, engagement data, and purchasing trends with analytics tools. You can use this data to get insightful insights that will help you improve customer experiences and your marketing campaigns.

Request Input
Ask for input from your clients on a regular basis to find out how satisfied they are and what needs to be improved. Inspire them to write testimonials and reviews, and interact with them on social media. By using this feedback loop, you may improve your connections with your target market and tailor your services to meet their demands.

In summary
One of the most important steps in creating a successful business is defining your target market. You may efficiently manage your resources, differentiate your firm, and adapt your marketing efforts by knowing and identifying your ideal

clientele. You can create strategies that connect with your customers and propel the expansion of your company by conducting in-depth market research and having a solid understanding of your target audience.

5.1 Establishing Your Goal Market

Identifying your target market is one of the most important phases of creating a profitable company. The particular client base that is most likely to be interested in your product or service is known as your target market. Knowing and identifying your target market can help you focus your marketing efforts and create methods that appeal to your ideal clients. This section will discuss the significance of identifying your target market and provide you with useful techniques for locating and comprehending your target demographic.

5.1.1 The Importance of Clearly Determining Your Target Market

It's critical to define your target market for a number of reasons. First of all, it enables you to concentrate your energies and resources on the clients who are most likely to buy your goods or services. Through comprehension of their requirements, inclinations, and actions, you may develop focused advertising strategies that successfully connect with and include your ideal clients.

Second, identifying your target market enables you to set your company apart from rivals. You may customize your product or service to match the unique needs of your target audience and differentiate yourself from the competition by learning what makes them unique. You may gain a competitive advantage and draw in devoted clients who identify with your brand by making this distinction.

Finally, having a clear understanding of your target market helps you spend your marketing money more wisely. Targeting a wide audience will only waste your efforts; instead, you should concentrate on the demographics most likely to become clients. Higher conversion rates and a better return on investment for your marketing efforts can result from this focused approach.

5.1.2 Determining Your Ideal Customer Base
You must collect pertinent data and carry out in-depth market research before you can define your target market. The following procedures can assist you in determining and comprehending your target audience:

Examine your product or service in step one.
Analyze your offering and determine its special qualities and advantages first. Think about the issue it resolves, the value it provides, and the ways it differs from competing products in the market.

You may better grasp the precise wants and desires that your product or service satisfies with the use of this investigation.

Step 2: Do industry research.
To learn more about consumer preferences, market trends, and the competitive environment, conduct industry research. Find out about the market's size, potential for growth, and important players. Your comprehension of market dynamics will expand as a result of this research, which will also assist you in recognizing possibilities and difficulties.

Step 3: Describe the Demographic Features
Aspects including age, gender, economic bracket, degree of education, and occupation are examples of demographic features. To ascertain which demographic groups are most likely to be interested in what you have to offer, analyze your product or service. If you are a premium skincare product seller, for instance, your target market can be composed of well-to-do people in their 30s to 50s who have more money to spend.

Step 4: Take Psychographic Aspects into Account
The psychological and lifestyle traits of your target audience are the main focus of psychographic variables. Take into account their values, habits, interests, and attitudes. For example, if you sell eco-friendly products, those that value sustainability and the environment can be part of your target market.

Step 5: Perform interviews and surveys.
Consider interviewing and surveying potential customers to gain more detailed information about your target market. Inquire about their inclinations, purchasing patterns, and problems. You will gain insightful knowledge from this primary research and be able to better grasp your target audience.

Step 6: Examine the clients of competitors
Examine the clientele of your rivals to learn more about their intended audience. Look for trends and parallels in their clientele. You can target underserved or possible holes in the market with the aid of this analysis.

5.1.3 Recognizing Your Ideal Clientele
Understanding your target market's demands, motives, and behaviors in great detail is essential after you've determined who they are. Your marketing tactics will be informed by this knowledge, which will also enable you to craft messages that effectively appeal to your target market. The following are some strategies to help you comprehend your target market better:

Perform market analysis.
To keep abreast of the most recent developments and trends in your target market, keep up your market research. Keep an eye on trade periodicals, visit trade exhibitions, and conduct focus groups and surveys with your target market. This continuous research will assist you in modifying

your tactics to satisfy changing client demands.

Make personas for buyers.
Create fictionalized versions of your ideal clients, or buyer personas. These personas must contain specific pain areas and goals, along with psychographic traits and demographic data. You may better understand your target market and adjust your marketing messaging by developing thorough buyer personas.

Examine client information.
Utilize customer data to learn more about the habits and preferences of your target market. Track website traffic, engagement data, and purchasing trends with analytics tools. You can use this data to get insightful insights that will help you improve customer experiences and your marketing campaigns.

Request Input
Ask for input from your clients on a regular basis to find out how satisfied they are and what needs to be improved. Inspire them to write testimonials and reviews, and interact with them on social media. By using this feedback loop, you may improve your connections with your target market and tailor your services to meet their demands.

In summary
One of the most important steps in creating a successful business is defining your target market.

You may efficiently manage your resources, differentiate your firm, and adapt your marketing efforts by knowing and identifying your ideal clientele. You can create strategies that connect with your customers and propel the expansion of your company by conducting in-depth market research and having a solid understanding of your target audience.

5.2 Crafting a Strong Corporate Identity

The heart and soul of your company lie in your brand identity. It is what distinguishes you from your rivals and leaves a lasting effect on your intended market. This section will go over the essential components of developing a strong and distinctive brand identity that connects with your target audience.

5.2.1 Establishing the Character of Your Brand

Identifying your brand's personality is a prerequisite to developing a strong brand identity. The human qualities and attributes that you wish people to identify with your brand are known as its personality. It influences how your brand engages and communicates with your target market.

Start by asking yourself these important questions to help you define your brand's personality:

What are your company's guiding principles and beliefs?

What impression do you want your target market to have of your brand?

Which feelings do you want consumers to associate with your brand?

Which essential qualities and traits best describe your brand?

You can begin to have a clear idea of the personality you want your brand to represent by providing answers to these questions. This will be the starting point for developing an engaging brand identity.

5.2.2 Telling the Story of Your Brand

Every well-known brand has an interesting backstory. What establishes a stronger connection between your audience and your company is your brand story. With your customers, it fosters an emotional bond and increases trust.

Take into account these components when creating your brand story:

Your beginnings: Tell the tale of how your company got started. What motivated you to launch this business? Which obstacles did you surmount along the way?

Your goals and objectives: Express your vision and purpose statements clearly. What is your company's mission? What goals do you have in mind?

Your principles: Determine the guiding principles

of your company. Which values do you uphold? How does the identity of your brand reflect these values?

What makes you stand out from the competition? Emphasize what makes your company unique compared to the competition. What distinguishes your goods or services from others? How does it address a market need or solve an issue?

Combining these components will allow you to craft an engaging brand narrative that will appeal to your target market and set your company apart from its competitors.

5.2.3 Creating a Visual Brand
Your brand is visually represented by your visual identity. It consists of your typeface, color scheme, logo, and other visual components that support the development of a unified and consistent brand image.

When creating your visual brand, keep the following in mind:

The most identifiable aspect of your brand is your logo. It needs to be straightforward, memorable, and encapsulate the essence of your company.

Color scheme: Select a scheme that reflects the essence of your brand and arouses the feelings you want in your target market. Make an informed choice because different colors have distinct psychological effects.

Typography: Choose readable typefaces that capture the essence of your company. To add visual interest, think about combining different fonts.

Imagery: Select visuals and graphics that appeal to your target market and are consistent with the essence of your brand. Make use of excellent images that successfully communicate the message of your brand.

You can make a lasting impact on your audience by developing a visually appealing and recognizable brand identity.

5.2.4 Developing Your Brand's Tone

The tone and communication style you employ to interact with your audience are known as your brand voice. It should convey the essence of your brand and be consistent throughout all of your marketing platforms.

As you develop your brand voice, keep the following in mind:

Tone: Choose the voice that most embodies your brand. Is the tone casual or formal? Is it lighthearted or serious? Friendly or authoritative?

Phasing: Select words and phrases that appeal to your intended audience. Take into account their values, preferences, and demographics.

Messaging: Create essential messages that appeal to your audience and are consistent with the ideals of your brand. Every single one of your marketing products should carry the same message.

You can establish a solid and genuine relationship with your audience by developing a distinctive and dependable brand voice.

5.2.5 Regularity Is Essential
Being consistent is essential to creating a memorable brand identity. From your website and social media accounts to your packaging and customer support, your brand should be the same everywhere.

Maintain uniformity by:

Establishing brand guidelines: Write a set of rules that specify how your brand should be spoken and visually portrayed. This covers standards for the use of the logo, color scheme, font, and voice.
Educating your group: Inform the members of your team of your brand's guidelines and identity. Make sure that the essence and core principles of your brand are understood and embraced by all.
Keeping an eye on and imposing consistency: Make sure all of your marketing collateral and touchpoints are consistent with your brand identity by reviewing them frequently. To keep things consistent, make the necessary adjustments.
You can develop a powerful and identifiable brand that connects with your audience and distinguishes you from your rivals by being consistent.

In the following part, we'll look at some efficient marketing techniques to build your brand and draw in clients.

5.3 Formulating Powerful Marketing Plans

Any firm that wants to reach its target audience, increase brand awareness, and eventually boost sales needs to focus on marketing. We'll look at the essential components of creating marketing plans that work in this section and will help your company grow. You will discover how to develop an all-encompassing marketing strategy that complements your company objectives, from identifying your target market to developing a persuasive message and putting various marketing channels into action.

5.3.1 Establishing Your Goal Market

It's crucial to identify your target market precisely before you can promote your goods or services. The particular set of people or companies that are most likely to be interested in what you have to offer is your target market. Understanding their requirements, inclinations, and habits will help you design marketing campaigns that will appeal to them.

Doing market research is the first step in defining your target market. This entails learning as much as you can about your potential clients' psychographics—their interests, values, and way of life—and demographics—their age, gender, and region. This information can be gathered through surveys, interviews, or by examining already-published market research studies.

After gathering the required data, develop buyer personas. These are fictitious depictions of your ideal clientele, created using the information you have gathered. Details like age, occupation, aspirations, problems, and preferred communication routes should all be included in each buyer's persona. Knowing your target market well will help you make more informed marketing decisions and craft communications that will appeal to them.

5.3.2 Establishing a Strong Brand Identity

Building consumer loyalty and standing out in a crowded market require a strong brand identity. The visual components, message, and core values that characterize your company and set it apart from rivals make up your brand identity. It is what distinguishes you and gives your company a lasting impression.

Establishing your company's mission and values is the first step towards developing a strong brand identity. What values do you uphold? What is your company's mission? The tone and message of your brand will be determined by these fundamental components. Next, create a distinctive brand voice that appeals to and resonates with your target audience. Your brand voice should be the same across all marketing platforms, no matter how serious, lighthearted, or authoritative it is.

A logo, color scheme, and typography are examples of visual components that are important to brand identity. Select typefaces and colors that speak to your target audience and convey the individuality of your brand. Your logo needs to be uncomplicated, distinctive, and instantly identifiable. Maintaining visual coherence in all of your marketing collateral will help your audience recognize and associate your brand with you more easily.

5.3.3 Creating Powerful Channels for Marketing

It's time to build efficient marketing channels to reach your audience when you have identified your target market and developed a strong brand identity. Online and offline, there are a variety of marketing channels to select from, so make sure they complement your target market and business objectives.

Channels for internet marketing consist of:

Website: Your website acts as the focal point of all of your marketing initiatives and is the online representation of your company. Make sure your website is optimized for search engines, visually appealing, and easy to use.

Search Engine Optimization (SEO): To rank higher in search engine results, you must optimize your website and content. You may increase your website's exposure and draw in organic traffic by using pertinent keywords, producing excellent content, and developing backlinks.

Social media: You may interact with your target audience, publish insightful material, and increase brand awareness by using social media sites like Facebook, Instagram, Twitter, and LinkedIn. Select the most well-liked platforms for your intended audience and create a regular posting schedule.

Email marketing: Creating an email list enables you to interact with your audience directly and develop lasting connections. To keep your subscribers interested and informed about your goods or services, send out newsletters, specials, and tailored material on a regular basis.

Channels for offline marketing consist of:

Print Advertising: Certain target markets can still be effectively reached by traditional print advertising, such as advertisements in newspapers, magazines, and brochures. When choosing options for print advertising, take your audience's tastes and demographics into account.

Events and Sponsorships: You may reach a specific audience and increase brand awareness by taking part in trade exhibits, industry events, or sponsoring neighborhood gatherings. During these events, networking can also result in beneficial collaborations and partnerships.

Direct Mail: You can effectively capture your target audience's attention and direct them to your website or physical store by sending them physical mail, such as catalogs or postcards.

When creating your marketing channels, it's critical to monitor and evaluate each channel's performance to ascertain its efficacy. Measure website traffic, social media engagement, email open rates, and conversion rates with analytics tools. You may use this information to make well-informed decisions about which channels to focus more on and which ones might benefit from tweaks.

5.3.4 Creating Marketing Messages That Are Powerful

It is now time to create persuasive marketing messages that connect with your audience after you have determined who your target market is and which marketing channels are best for you. Your marketing communications should make it apparent to your target audience why they should pick you over rivals, as well as the advantages and worth of your goods and services.

Take into account the following advice while creating persuasive marketing messages:

Pay attention to the benefits: Emphasize the particular advantages that your target market can obtain from your products or services. How will they better their lives or find solutions to their problems? Express your offerings' value proposition and distinctive selling features in a clear and concise manner.

Employ Emotional Appeal: Using relatable stories and storytelling, appeal to the emotions of your target audience. In your marketing messaging, try to arouse emotions such as happiness, security, or success, as these can be strong motivators for buying decisions.

Keep It Simple: Steer clear of technical terms or jargon that could alienate or confuse your readers. Make sure your language is understandable and succinct, and concentrate on the main ideas that will appeal to your target audience.

Incorporate social proof to establish credibility and trust, including case studies, customer testimonials, or reviews. Any skepticism or worries your target market may have regarding your goods or services can be allayed with the aid of social proof.

Formulate a call to action that makes it obvious

what you want the people who will be reading your marketing materials to do. A compelling call to action will direct your audience to do the desired action, which could be buying something, subscribing to your newsletter, or getting in touch with you for further details.

Your marketing campaigns will be more effective and generate more conversions if you create captivating marketing messages that relate to the needs and desires of your target market.

In summary, creating a successful marketing strategy is critical to your company's success. You may effectively reach and engage your audience by defining your target market, developing a compelling brand identity, selecting the appropriate marketing channels, and generating appealing marketing messaging. In order to enhance your plans and make data-driven decisions, don't forget to consistently monitor and assess the outcomes of your marketing campaigns.

5.4 Putting Sales Techniques and Strategies into Practice

In the realm of business, sales are essential to the expansion and success of any enterprise. Even the most inventive and exciting concepts may find it difficult to acquire traction in the market without strong sales tactics and methods. This part will go over the essential ideas and methods that will enable you to put effective sales tactics and plans into action in order to increase sales and advance your company.

5.4.1 Gaining Knowledge of the Sales Process

A thorough grasp of the sales process is essential before delving into certain sales tactics and methods. Prospecting, qualifying leads, presenting your product or service, addressing objections, completing the deal, and maintaining client relationships are some of the steps that make up the traditional sales process. Each step calls for a different set of abilities and methods;

by comprehending this process, you'll have the foundation you need to apply sales tactics and strategies successfully.

5.4.2 Establishing Robust Connections with Clients

Developing a solid rapport with your clients is one of the cornerstones of successful sales. Customers are more inclined to purchase from someone they get along well with and trust. It is crucial to concentrate on offering value, comprehending your clients' demands, and providing outstanding customer service if you want to develop long-lasting relationships with them. Going above and beyond to satisfy your clients' needs can help you build enduring connections that encourage recurring business and positive word-of-mouth recommendations.

5.4.3 Determining and Aiming for Your Perfect Clients

Finding and pursuing your targeted clientele is crucial if you want to increase revenue. To do this, you must carry out market research to ascertain the characteristics, inclinations, and problems of your target market. You can adjust your sales tactics and methods to effectively express the value of your good or service by getting to know your consumers' requirements and motivations. You can focus on the prospects who have the highest likelihood of becoming paying customers and spend your resources more effectively by identifying and targeting your ideal clientele.

5.4.4 Crafting Powerful Sales Demonstrations

Making powerful sales presentations is a crucial component of putting successful sales tactics and strategies into practice. A well-made sales presentation should address the concerns of your target audience, highlight the special value proposition of your good or service, and show how it can help them. It's critical to use language and graphics in your sales presentations that speak to your target audience's unique requirements and preferences. Furthermore, using storytelling tactics can help you connect emotionally with your audience and leave a lasting impression on them.

5.4.5 Overcoming Disagreements and Managing Turndowns

Rejections and objections are commonplace in the sales process. Nonetheless, proficient sales professionals possess the ability to surmount objections and manage rejections in a constructive and optimistic way. When presented with objections, it's critical to pay attention to what your clients are saying, understand where they're coming from, and thoughtfully address any issues they may have. It's also critical to see rejections as teaching moments rather than as indications of one's own shortcomings. Examine the reasons behind the rejection, get input, and apply it to improve your sales methods and approaches.

5.4.6 Making Use of Technology to Automate Sales

In the digital age we live in today, technology is important for sales. Lead generation, customer relationship management, and sales analytics are just a few of the areas of the sales process that sales automation technologies can help to enhance and streamline. Through the use of technology, you may increase productivity, obtain insightful knowledge about your sales success, and automate tedious operations. Finding a balance between personalization and automation is crucial, though. Technology might help you in sales, but it should never take the place of a personal touch and tailored interactions with your clients.

5.4.7 Ongoing Education and Adjustment

Strategies and tactics for selling don't stay the same; they change as the market and consumer demands do. Adopting an attitude of constant learning and adaptability is essential to staying ahead of the competition. Attend sales training sessions, stay current on industry developments, and ask for and receive feedback from peers and clients. You can make sure that your strategy stays current and successful in a company environment that is constantly changing by consistently improving and modifying your sales approaches and strategies.

5.4.8 Assessing and Examining Sales Results

Measuring and analyzing your sales success is crucial to determining how well your tactics and strategy are working. Conversion rates, average deal size, and client acquisition cost are a few examples of key performance indicators (KPIs) that can give you important information about how well your sales efforts are doing. Make data-driven decisions by tracking and analyzing these indicators on a regular basis to find areas for development and streamline your sales process.

Putting into practice successful sales tactics and strategies is crucial to your company's development and success. You can improve your sales efforts and increase revenue for your business by comprehending the sales process, fostering strong customer relationships, identifying your ideal clients, creating persuasive sales presentations, overcoming obstacles, utilizing technology, accepting continuous learning, and tracking sales performance. Recall that sales is about more than just making sales; it's also about earning your clients' confidence, attending to their needs, and providing value.

Building a Strong Online

Presence

6.1 Developing an Easy-to-Use Website

A solid online presence is crucial for every organization to succeed in the modern digital era. The cornerstone of your online presence is a user-friendly website that functions as a virtual storefront, showcasing your goods and services to prospective clients. It is essential to design a website that offers a smooth and simple user experience in addition to an eye-catching aesthetic. The essential components and recommended procedures for developing a user-friendly website that will draw in and keep your target audience are covered in this section.

6.1.1 Realizing How Important User-Friendliness Is

The requirements and tastes of the users are taken into consideration when designing a user-friendly website. Its main goal is to give users a satisfying experience by making it simple for them to navigate, locate information, and complete desired tasks. A user-friendly website improves user satisfaction overall, tempts visitors to stay on it longer, and raises the possibility of conversions. Furthermore, as search engines give preference to websites that provide an excellent user experience, having a user-friendly website might raise its search engine rankings.

6.1.2 Identifying the Objectives and Target Market for Your Website

Determining your target audience and defining your website's goals are essential steps before beginning the design and development process. It will be easier for you to decide what features and functionalities your website needs when you are aware of your goals. For instance, you would require an e-commerce platform that is incorporated into your website if your objective is to sell things online. By determining who your target audience is, you can adjust the content and design of your website to better suit their interests and requirements.

6.1.3 Organizing the Navigation and Structure of the Website

The foundation of a user-friendly website is clear navigation and a well-organized structure. Make a sitemap that lists the primary pages and subpages of your website as a starting point. This will assist you in seeing the information's flow and hierarchy. Keep the navigation menu's design straightforward and understandable. Make sure that each menu item has a clear and succinct label so that users can quickly and easily locate what they're looking for.

6.1.4 Creating a User-Friendly and Adaptable Layout

Your website's visual design is very important for drawing in visitors and communicating your company's identity. Select a design that complements the aesthetics of your brand and is clear and polished. Make use of eye-catching visuals and photos that are pertinent to your company. Make sure your website is responsive, which means it can adjust to various screen sizes and gadgets. It's crucial to give consumers who visit your website on smartphones and tablets a flawless experience because mobile devices are becoming more and more common.

6.1.5 Improving the Loading Speed of Websites

Users have little patience for slow-loading websites in today's fast-paced world. Improving the speed at which your website loads is essential to giving users a satisfying experience. Reduce the size of files and photos without sacrificing quality by compressing them. Use as few plugins and scripts as possible to avoid making your website load more slowly. Reduce the amount of time it takes for pages to load by using caching techniques to store frequently visited material. Maintain regular performance monitoring and optimization of your website to guarantee quick loading times.

6.1.6 Producing Interesting and Useful Content
Engaging website visitors and motivating them to take action require compelling and pertinent information. Provide attention-grabbing headlines that succinctly express your company's value proposition. Make use of enlightening and convincing writing that shows the advantages of your goods or services and speaks to the concerns of your target market. To improve the visual appeal and communicate information in a more engaging way, include visuals like photos, videos, and infographics.

6.1.7 Putting Intuitive Forms and Calls to Action into Practice
The use of forms and calls-to-action (CTAs) is essential for transforming website visitors into leads or paying clients. Create forms that are simple to complete, with few required fields and clear instructions. Strategically place calls to action (CTAs) throughout your website,

drawing attention using eye-catching content and contrasting colors. Make sure CTAs are simple to click through and direct users to the intended action, which could be buying something, subscribing to a newsletter, or asking for additional details.

6.1.8 Including Techniques for Search Engine Optimization (SEO)

SEO strategies must be used if you want to make sure that search engines can find your website and that it gets natural traffic. Find appropriate keywords by conducting keyword research, then organically integrate them into the content of your website. To increase the exposure of your website in search engine results, optimize your meta tags, including title tags and meta descriptions. Produce readable, aesthetically pleasing material that will draw in backlinks from reliable sources to raise your search engine results even further.

6.1.9 Evaluation and Ongoing Enhancement

A user-friendly website must be continuously tested and improved, which is a continual process. To find areas for improvement and get input from actual users, conduct usability studies. Keep an eye on your website's analytics to learn more about user behavior and make informed decisions. Make sure that the functionality, design, and content of your website are updated and optimized on a regular basis to keep it user-friendly and in line with the changing needs of your target audience.

By implementing these best practices and concentrating on developing a user-friendly website, you can provide your visitors with a satisfying online experience, boost engagement, and eventually propel your company's success. Recall that your website is an effective tool that has the potential to greatly affect both your customer acquisition and brand reputation. Take the time and make the necessary investments to develop a website that engages your target audience, embodies the values of your brand, and advances your business objectives.

6.2 Search Engine Optimization (SEO) Implementation

In the current digital era, a company's ability to succeed online depends heavily on its online presence. Making sure your website stands out and draws in the correct audience is crucial because there are millions of websites vying for users' attention. This is where SEO, or search engine optimization, is useful. Optimizing your website to increase its exposure and rating on search engine results pages (SERPs) is known as search engine optimization (SEO). You may enhance organic website traffic, produce leads, and eventually propel business expansion by putting SEO tactics into practice.

6.2.1 Gaining an Overview of SEO Fundamentals
It's crucial to comprehend the fundamental ideas guiding SEO before delving into its complexities. When consumers search for particular keywords or phrases, search engines like Google utilize sophisticated algorithms to assess the quality and relevancy of websites. You can increase the likelihood that your website will rank higher on SERPs by being aware of these algorithms and optimizing it appropriately.

Researching keywords is a crucial component of SEO. Finding the terms and phrases that members of your target market are probably going to use to look for goods or services comparable to yours is part of this process. You may improve your website's search engine exposure by carefully choosing the keywords to use in the meta tags, URLs, and content of your pages.

On-page SEO is another crucial component of SEO. To make your website more search engine-friendly, you must optimize its many components, including headings, title tags, meta descriptions, and picture alt tags. You may raise your website's search engine rating by making sure these components appropriately represent the content of your website and contain pertinent keywords.

6.2.2 Making exceptional and interesting content
The caliber and applicability of a website's content are two of the most crucial aspects that search engines take into account when ranking webpages. Creating excellent, educational, and captivating content is good for search engine optimization as well as for the users of your website.

It's crucial to concentrate on offering your audience value while producing content for your website. This can be achieved through attending to their issues, responding to their inquiries, and providing solutions. You can become an authority in your field and draw a devoted following by regularly producing high-quality material.

Not only should great material be produced, but it should also be search engine optimized. You can achieve this by employing headers and subheadings that are descriptive, including pertinent keywords organically in your text, and providing both internal and external links to reliable sources. You may raise your content's visibility and chances of ranking higher on SERPs by adhering to these best practices.

6.2.3 Establishing Trusted Backlinks

Backlinks are links pointing to your website from other websites; they are also referred to as inbound links. Backlinks are regarded by search engines as a sign of the authority and relevancy of your website. Your website will rank better in search engine results with the more high-quality backlinks it has.

It takes strategy to build backlinks of the highest caliber. An efficient tactic is to get in contact with other websites within your sector and propose to write articles or guest posts. Backlinks to your own website can be obtained by contributing valuable material to these websites. It's critical to concentrate on domain-authority-rich and industry-relevant websites.

Making shareable content that gets backlinks organically is another successful tactic. This can be achieved through the publication of in-depth manuals or tutorials, the creation of infographics, or original research. Through social media and other channels, you can draw backlinks from other websites and make this material more visible.

6.2.4 Tracking and Examining SEO Outcomes

Applying SEO tactics is a continuous process. Making sure your efforts are producing the appropriate results requires ongoing observation and analysis. You may obtain important insights into your website's traffic, user activity, and conversion rates by routinely monitoring its performance using tools like Google Analytics.

You may find areas for development and make data-driven decisions by analyzing the performance of your website. You can improve your content further to more successfully target specific keywords, for instance, if you see that they are bringing in a lot of traffic to your website. Likewise, you can modify pages to enhance the user experience if you observe a high bounce rate on specific pages.

It's critical to stay current with SEO trends and algorithm changes in addition to tracking the functionality of your website. To give consumers the most relevant and superior search results, search engines are always improving their algorithms. Your website's search engine ranking can be sustained and even increased by keeping up with the latest developments and modifying your SEO tactics accordingly.

In conclusion
Building a solid online presence and drawing the correct kind of visitors to your website depend on the application of efficient SEO techniques. You can boost your website's visibility, expand organic traffic, and spur business growth by learning the fundamentals of SEO, producing interesting and high-quality content, constructing high-quality backlinks, and tracking and evaluating its effectiveness. Recall that in order to stay ahead of the competition, SEO is a continual process that

demands constant effort and modification.

6.3 Using Social Media to Advance Your Company

Social media has become an essential component of our everyday lives in the current digital era. It has completely changed how we connect, communicate, and use information. Using social media channels to your advantage as an entrepreneur can revolutionize the way your company grows. It gives you an effective tool to connect with and interact with your target market, increase brand recognition, and increase website traffic. We will look at several tactics and best practices in this part for using social media to propel your company's expansion.

6.3.1 Selecting Appropriate Social Media Networks

With so many social media channels at your disposal, it's critical to select the ones that complement your target market and business objectives. It's important to understand the interests and behaviors of your audience because every platform has different features and user demographics. The following are some well-known social media sites, along with their salient features:

Facebook: The biggest social media network, with over 2.8 billion monthly active users, is Facebook. It is appropriate for companies of all sizes because it provides a broad range of targeting choices and advertising capabilities.

Instagram: Known for its eye-catching aesthetic, Instagram is a very interactive network that's great for businesses, especially those in the fashion, beauty, and lifestyle sectors. Additionally, it provides a range of advertising choices, such as carousel, picture, and video advertisements.

Twitter: Businesses may share news and updates in real time and participate in conversations on this fast-paced medium. Businesses in the tech, news, and entertainment sectors find it especially beneficial.

LinkedIn: LinkedIn is a business- and professional-focused professional networking site. It is the perfect venue for thought leadership, recruitment, and B2B companies.

YouTube: Businesses can produce and distribute video content on YouTube, which is the second-largest search engine behind Google. It works especially well for companies in the instructional, educational, and entertainment sectors.

TikTok: Short-form video creation and sharing are made possible by this quickly expanding platform. It is well-liked by younger audiences and can provide firms aiming to market to Generation Z with a superb platform.

Recall that not all social networking platforms require your presence. Concentrate on the channels where you can generate significant interaction with your target audience.

6.3.2 Formulating a Plan for Social Media

Having a clearly defined social media plan is crucial for utilizing social media for business growth. Take into consideration these crucial steps:

Establish Specific Objectives: Establish your objectives for social media: are they to raise brand awareness, increase website traffic, generate leads, or enhance customer engagement? Your objectives will direct your social media activities and assist in gauging your progress.

Know Your Audience: Recognize the characteristics, passions, and online habits of your target market. With this information, you can better craft messaging and content that appeals to your target demographic.

Produce Captivating Content: Formulate a content plan that is consistent with your brand and appeals to your target market. To keep your audience interested, blend promotional, educational, and amusing content.

Keys to Maintaining an Active Presence on Social Media: Consistency is essential. For a regular flow of material, create a content calendar and plan your posts ahead of time.

Engage Your Audience: Developing relationships with your audience is equally as important as spreading your message on social media. React as soon as possible to mentions, messages, and comments. Encourage user-generated material, hold contests, and pose questions to your audience to keep them interested.

Analyze and Monitor: Using the analytics tools offered by each platform, keep a close eye on your social media performance on a regular basis. Examine the statistics to see what kind of information appeals to your audience, then modify your approach accordingly.

6.3.3 Social Media Paid Promotion
Even if social media organic reach is important, paid advertising can greatly expand your audience and hasten the expansion of your company. Social networking sites provide a range of advertising choices to accommodate varying goals and budgets. Here are a few well-liked solutions for paid advertising:

Facebook Advertising: Facebook provides a wide range of ad forms, such as picture, video, carousel, and lead generation ads, as part of its all-inclusive advertising platform. By enabling you to target particular demographics, hobbies, and behaviors, you can make sure the correct people see your ads.

Instagram Ads: Facebook Ads Manager is the tool used to design and manage Instagram ads. A variety of ad forms are available for selection, such as story, carousel, picture, and video ads. Instagram is great for showcasing products and increasing conversions because of its visual format.

LinkedIn Ads: Professionals can target ads on LinkedIn according to their industry, interests, and job titles. It works especially well for B2B companies trying to increase brand awareness and lead generation among industry experts.

Twitter Ads: Promoted tweets, promoted accounts, and promoted trends are just a few of the advertising opportunities that Twitter provides. To reach your intended audience, it enables you to target particular keywords, interests, and demographics.

YouTube advertising: YouTube provides a variety of ad forms, such as overlay advertising, sponsored cards, and both skippable and non-skippable video ads. Users can be targeted according to their search history, interests, and demographics.

To maximize your return on investment, it's critical to establish precise goals, specify your target market, and keep an eye on the effectiveness of your advertisements while executing paid advertising campaigns.

6.3.4 Influencer Promotion

In recent years, influencer marketing has become incredibly popular. It entails working together with well-known people on social media to market your goods and services. Influencers can help you gain credibility and reach a larger audience because they have a devoted fan base. The following actions should be taken into account while doing influencer marketing:

Find Relevant Influencers: Do your homework and find influencers who share the same values as your target market, industry, and brand. Seek out influencers who have a loyal and involved fan base.

Form a partnership: Get in touch with influential people and suggest working together. Make sure that all of the partnership's terms—such as the kind of content, deliverables, and payment—are clearly stated.

Provide genuine material: Give influencers the creative freedom to produce material that speaks to their audience and advances your business. Establishing trust with their followers requires authenticity.

Track and Measure Outcomes: Utilizing distinct landing pages, discount coupons, or trackable links, keep an eye on the effectiveness of influencer efforts. Examine the information to see how influencer marketing has affected your company.

Keep in mind that sincerity and transparency are essential while collaborating with influencers. Make sure influencers reveal their relationship with your brand in order to uphold transparency and adhere to advertising laws.

6.3.5 Involving Your Viewers

Social media is a great way to interact with your audience and create lasting connections. The following are some methods to increase involvement:

React to Messages and Comments: Invest some time in giving prompt attention to any messages, comments, and mentions. Demonstrate to your audience that you are attentive to their comments and that you value them.

Promote user-generated content: Motivate people in your audience to produce and distribute brand-related content. Testimonials, evaluations, or imaginative material showcasing your goods or services can fall under this category. User-generated content broadens your audience and fosters trust.

Organize giveaways and contests. These are excellent ways to spark interest and enthusiasm. Offer incentives to your audience, like discounts, freebies, or special access, to entice them to join.

Organize live Q&A sessions: These sessions provide you the chance to communicate with your audience in real time. It's an opportunity to respond to their questions, offer insightful commentary, and demonstrate your experience.

Provide Behind-the-Scenes Content: By providing behind-the-scenes content, you can give your audience an inside look at your company. These might be staff spotlights, office tours, or advance looks at new items. It makes your brand more relatable and creates a feeling of community.

Recall that social media is a channel for two-way communication. Actively interact with your audience, pay attention to their opinions, and offer something of value to create a devoted following for your business.

In summary
In today's digital economy, using social media for business growth is a must, not an option. You may use social media to advance your brand by selecting the appropriate platforms, creating a strong plan, employing influencer marketing, using paid advertising, and interacting with your audience. Accept the chances that social media offers and see how your company prospers in the virtual sphere.

6.4 Making Use of Content Marketing Techniques
Content marketing has become a vital tool for organizations in the modern digital age to communicate with their target audience, increase brand awareness, and boost sales. Through the production and dissemination of content that is meaningful, relevant, and consistent, businesses may become leaders in their sector and build a devoted clientele. We'll look at a variety of content marketing techniques in this area to help you reach your marketing objectives and market your company successfully.

6.4.1 Realizing Content Marketing's Significance
There is more to content marketing than merely writing blog entries and social media updates. It's a calculated tactic that centers on producing and disseminating worthwhile content in order to draw in and hold on to a target audience. Businesses can build credibility and trust with their target audience by offering pertinent and

helpful information; this will eventually lead to a rise in customer loyalty and sales.

The capacity of content marketing to inform and educate consumers is one of its main advantages. By offering insightful advice, industry knowledge, and helpful hints, companies may establish themselves as authorities in their sector and win over their audience's trust. Increased brand loyalty and consumer retention may result from this trust.

Furthermore, content marketing enables companies to highlight their distinct value proposition and set themselves apart from rivals. By producing material that accentuates their areas of expertise, offerings, or services, companies can draw in clients who are specifically searching for their services.

6.4.2 Formulating a Plan for Content Marketing

A clear strategy must be developed in order to use content marketing effectively. The objectives, target audience, content kinds, distribution methods, and success measures are all outlined in a content marketing strategy. When creating your content marketing plan, keep the following important steps in mind:

6.4.2.1 Establish Your Objectives

Establish your objectives for content marketing first. Are you trying to build thought leadership, drive website traffic, create leads, or raise brand awareness? You can coordinate your content strategy to accomplish your goals by identifying them.

6.4.2.2 Determine Who Your Target Market Is

To create content that appeals to your target audience, you must have a thorough understanding of them. To find out their preferences, pain points, hobbies, and demographics, conduct market research. You can use this information to better customize your content to their interests and requirements.

6.4.2.3 Select the appropriate content categories.

You can produce a variety of content formats, such as case studies, podcasts, infographics, films, blog articles, and whitepapers. To choose the content types that will most effectively reach and engage your audience, take into account the preferences of your target audience as well as the specifics of your organization.

6.4.2.4 Choose the Appropriate Channels for Distribution

After producing your content, you must choose the most effective distribution channels. Your website, blog, social media accounts, email newsletters, trade journals, and guest posts on pertinent websites are a few examples of this. Select channels that correspond with the inclinations and behaviors of your intended audience.

6.4.2.5 Establish a Content Calendar

You can maintain consistency and organization in the production and distribution of your content by creating a content calendar. To guarantee your audience receives high-quality information on a consistent basis, schedule your content subjects, formats, and release dates in advance.

6.4.2.6 Measure and Examine Outcomes

Keep an eye on and evaluate the results of your content marketing campaigns on a regular basis. To assess the success of your content strategy, monitor indicators like website traffic, conversions, social media shares, and engagement rates. Make wise decisions and improve your future content by using this data.

6.4.3 Producing Useful and Interesting Content

Content needs to be valuable, relevant, and engaging in order to engage readers and get results. The following advice can help you produce engaging content:

6.4.3.1 Recognize the Needs of Your Audience

Consider your audience from their point of view before producing any material. What answers or information are they looking for? What difficulties do they encounter? Knowing what they need can help you provide content that solves their problems and offers insightful information.

6.4.3.2 Offer Useful Information

Your writing should provide your audience with

doable solutions, suggestions, or guidance. You establish yourself as a reliable source and raise the possibility of audience participation and exchange by offering practical ideas.

6.4.3.3 Make Use of Images and Videos

Adding visual elements to your material, including photos, videos, infographics, and slideshows, can help it become more interesting and memorable. Images aid in breaking up words and presenting information in a way that is easier to understand.

6.4.3.4 Tell Tales

An effective technique for holding an audience's interest and establishing an emotional bond is storytelling. Employ narrative strategies to present case studies, customer success stories, or real-world examples that highlight the benefits of your goods or services.

6.4.3.5 Make Your Content Search Engine Friendly

Make sure your material is search engine-optimized to ensure it reaches a larger audience. Find suitable keywords by conducting keyword research, then organically integrate them into your writing. This will raise your website's organic traffic and search engine rankings.

6.4.4 How to Market and Share Your Content

Producing outstanding content is just half the battle. You must distribute and advertise it wisely if you want to maximize its impact. Here are some tactics to think about:

6.4.4.1 Promotion on Social Media

Make use of social media channels to interact with your audience and distribute your material. Make engaging social media postings that draw attention to the main ideas in your writing and entice readers to visit your website.

6.4.4.2 Email Promotion

To get your material in front of your readers directly, use email marketing. Distribute informative newsletters or content updates on a regular basis to engage readers and increase website traffic.

6.4.4.3 Outreach to Influencers

Find influential people in your field who have a sizable and devoted fan base. Work together to use their reach and credibility to promote your material to their audience.

6.4.4.4 Invited Bloggers

Contribute guest posts to respectable websites or trade journals that appeal to your intended readership. By doing this, you may capitalize on their current readership and position yourself as an authority in the field.

6.4.4.5 Sponsored Content

To reach a larger audience, think about employing paid advertising platforms like social media or Google Ads to market your content. In order to guarantee that the correct individuals see your material, target particular demographics or interests.

6.4.5 Examining and Improving Your Content Approach

Evaluate the results of your content marketing campaigns on a regular basis to determine what is effective and what requires improvement. Here are a few crucial metrics to monitor:

Traffic to the website and time spent there
Rate of bounces
Participation in social media
Rates of conversion
Make the most of your content strategy by using this data. Try out various themes, material forms, and distribution methods to see what your audience responds to the most. Make constant improvements to your material depending on the knowledge you have obtained from your analysis.

Effective use of content marketing techniques can help you build your brand, connect with your target market, and expand your company. In order to maximize your approach, never forget to regularly produce insightful and pertinent material, market it across a variety of platforms, and track its effectiveness. You can grow your business and meet your marketing objectives with a well-executed content marketing plan.

EFFECTIVE PRODUCT DEVELOPMENT

7.1 Comprehending the Process of Product Development

In the business world, the process of developing a product is an essential stage in realizing your idea. It entails turning your idea into a usable product that appeals to your target market's wants and demands. Entrepreneurs who wish to develop novel and profitable products must comprehend this process.

7.1.1 The Value of Developing New Products

Every successful company is built on the foundation of product development. It is the process of transforming a concept into a usable, concrete good that consumers may purchase. Your offering will be useful, distinct, and suit the needs of your target market if you put time and money into its creation.

Before releasing your product, the product development process enables you to polish your concept, recognize possible obstacles, and make the required adjustments. By providing something unique and superior to what is already on the market, it helps you get a competitive edge.

7.1.2 Product Development Stages

There are usually multiple stages in the product development process, each with specific goals and tasks. The following stages offer a general framework for comprehending the process, while the precise procedures may differ based on your product and business:

7.1.2.1 Generating Ideas

Idea generation is the initial step in the product development process. Here's where you generate concepts and ideas for your product through brainstorming. It entails determining issues or demands in the market and looking into creative fixes. Being creative and open-minded at this point is crucial, taking into account a range of options and viewpoints.

7.1.2.2 Analysis of Market Data

Undertake market research as soon as you have compiled a list of possible concepts. Getting knowledge of your target market, rivals, and market trends is part of this. You may find potential clients, gauge the market for your goods, and determine whether your ideas are viable with the aid of market research. Additionally, it gives you insights into customer preferences, enabling you to modify your product to suit their requirements.

7.1.2.3 Creation of Concepts

The process of honing your concepts and creating a distinct concept for your product is called concept development. This entails outlining the attributes, advantages, and value proposition of your offering. To visualize your idea and get input from possible clients, you can also make preliminary drawings or prototypes. Clarifying your vision and laying the groundwork for the subsequent phases of product development are two benefits of concept development.

7.1.2.4 Engineering and Design

The design and engineering phases start as soon as a concept is clearly established. Here's where you turn your idea into a comprehensive, producible design. To construct a prototype, it entails drafting technical specifications, carrying out feasibility studies, and working with engineers and designers. Your product will be both aesthetically beautiful and useful, meeting all necessary criteria thanks to design and engineering.

7.1.2.5 Evaluation and Recurrence

Iteration and testing are essential phases in the creation of new products. This is where you assess your prototype's usability, usefulness, and performance. You can find any bugs or areas that need work by doing thorough testing and making the required changes. You may improve your product and make sure it fulfills the demands and expectations of your target market by testing and iterating on it.

7.1.2.6 Production and Manufacturing

The stage of manufacturing and production starts when the design is complete. This includes locating supplies, establishing production procedures, and producing your product in large quantities. Establishing quality control procedures is crucial to making sure your product satisfies the necessary requirements. To guarantee prompt delivery and economical production, manufacturing and production demand meticulous planning and coordination.

7.1.2.7 Initiation and Marketing

Launching and commercializing your product is the last step in the product development process. This is the point at which you launch your product onto the market and begin to make sales. It includes creating promotional materials, establishing awareness within your target demographic, and formulating a marketing and sales strategy. Effective communication and distribution channels are essential for product launches and commercialization in order to reach clients and create demand.

7.1.3 Important Product Development Considerations

Entrepreneurs should have the following points in mind as they work through the product creation process:

7.1.3.1 A Customer-First Method

It's critical to keep the consumer at the center of the product development process. This entails comprehending the requirements and inclinations of your intended consumer base and developing your product in response. A product that meets and exceeds the expectations of the consumer can be made by placing the customer at the center of the decision-making process.

7.1.3.2 The Iterative Method

The process of developing a product is iterative. It entails obtaining feedback, iterative testing, and improvement. Adopting an iterative methodology enables you to modify and improve your work as needed in response to user input. Being flexible and willing to adjust can help you produce a product that develops and gets better with time.

7.1.3.3 Interdepartmental Cooperation

Effective product development necessitates cooperation between departments. It entails bringing together people with various specialties and backgrounds, including engineers, designers, marketers, and salesmen. You may use the expertise and abilities of your team as a whole to produce a successful and well-rounded product by encouraging team members to collaborate and communicate with one another.

7.1.3.4 Time and Expense Management

Effective time and cost management is essential to product development. Setting reasonable goals and deadlines and keeping a careful eye on them all during the process are crucial. Your product development can remain on schedule and under budget if you manage expenses and schedules well.

In summary

Entrepreneurs who wish to realize their ideas

must comprehend the process of product creation. You may effectively navigate the stages of product development by adhering to a methodical approach and taking important considerations into account. Recall to maintain a customer-focused mindset, adopt an iterative methodology, encourage cross-functional cooperation, and efficiently manage expenses and schedules. By doing this, you can raise your chances of developing a novel and successful product that appeals to your target market.

7.2 Researching the Market to Develop New Products

An essential phase in the creation of new products is market research. In order to decide on your product, you must collect and evaluate data on your target market, rivals, and market trends. You may determine consumer demands, evaluate market demand, and obtain insightful information that will direct your product development strategy by carrying out in-depth market research. This section will discuss the value of market research and provide you with useful advice on how to carry out efficient market research for your next project.

7.2.1 Recognizing the Value of Market Research

There are various reasons why market research is crucial. It assists you in comprehending your target market, determining the requirements and preferences of your customers, analyzing the competition, and gauging the demand for your product. You can do this by doing market research.

Determine your target market: Market research enables you to specify your target market and gain insight into the characteristics, habits, and preferences of your target audience. With this information, you can better customize your offering to their unique requirements and tastes.

Determine the needs of your customers: You may get important information about the wants and needs of your customers by holding focus groups, interviews, and surveys. Your product development process will be guided by this knowledge, which will also guarantee that the product addresses a legitimate need in your target market.

Analyze the competition: Market research enables you to comprehend the advantages, disadvantages, and positioning of your rivals. Through a thorough examination of their offerings, cost plans, and promotional methods, you can spot chances to set your product apart and obtain a competitive edge.

Analyze market demand: Determining the viability of your product requires an understanding of the size and development potential of your target market. You may evaluate consumer demand, spot market trends, and decide on price, distribution, and marketing tactics with the aid of market research.

7.2.2 Performing Primary Market Analysis
Directly gathering information from your target market is known as primary market research. Surveys, interviews, focus groups, and observations can all be used for this. To carry out efficient primary market research, follow these steps:

Specify the goals of your research: Clearly state the goals you have for your market research. Decide which precise questions you wish to address and what data you must collect.

Determine who your intended audience is. Ascertain your target audience's identity and your strategy for reaching them. Take into account variables like location, behavior, and demographics to make sure your research sample appropriately reflects your target market.

Select the research techniques you want to use: To acquire the information you require, choose the most suitable research techniques. While focus groups and interviews provide deeper qualitative insights, surveys are frequently used to gather quantitative data.

Create the tools for your research: Create discussion topics, interview guides, or questionnaires that support the goals of your study. For the purpose of collecting precise and significant data, make sure your questions are pertinent, objective, and unambiguous.

Gather information: Put your study strategy into action and acquire information from your intended audience. This could entail setting up focus groups, conducting interviews, or sending surveys. To get a variety of viewpoints, make sure the people you gather data from are varied.

Analyze and evaluate data: After gathering the information, examine it to find trends, patterns, and insights. To make sense of the data and come to relevant conclusions, apply qualitative coding techniques or statistical analysis tools.

Make decisions and develop conclusions. Determine your target market, client demands, and market demand based on your analysis. Make data-driven decisions and use these insights to guide your product development approach.

7.2.3 Carrying Out Secondary Market Analysis
Information from pre-existing sources, such as market studies, government publications, industry reports, and internet databases, is gathered for secondary market research. To carry out efficient secondary market research, follow these steps:

Determine pertinent sources: Ascertain which sources are most pertinent to your target market and industry. Seek reliable sources from government agencies, market research businesses, trade associations, and scholarly publications.

Collect information: Gather pertinent information and data from these sources. This could include competitive analysis, industry trends, market size, growth rates, and customer demographics. Make sure the information is accurate and current.

Analyze and interpret data: Look for important trends and insights by analyzing the data you have collected. Search for trends, openings in the industry, and other information that can help you with your product development plan.

Verify the results: To be sure your findings are accurate and trustworthy, cross-reference them with several sources. To get a complete picture of the market, compare data from other reports and research.

Incorporate insights into your approach to product development: Refine your product concept, spot market potential, and decide on price, positioning, and marketing tactics with the knowledge you've gathered from your secondary research.

7.2.4 Using Technology to Conduct Market Research

Technology has completely changed the manner in which market research is carried out. The following are some strategies for using technology to improve your market research:

Online surveys: To swiftly and affordably contact a large number of respondents, use online survey solutions. It's simple to create and distribute surveys with platforms like SurveyMonkey and Google Forms, and you can instantly evaluate the results.

Social media listening: Keep an eye on social media sites to learn about the attitudes, tastes, and trends of your customers. You can keep track of mentions, hashtags, and conversations pertaining to your business or product with the use of tools like Hootsuite and Sprout Social.

Web analytics: To collect information about website visitors, user behavior, and conversion rates, utilize web analytics solutions such as Google Analytics. By using this data, you may improve your online presence and gain insightful knowledge about the preferences of your customers.

Tools for competition analysis: Examine the web presence, traffic sources, and keyword ranks of your rivals using tools such as SEMrush and SimilarWeb. You can use this information to improve your product positioning and find market gaps.

Tools for data visualization: Use Tableau or Infogram to visualize the results of your market study. Making better judgments is made possible by data visualization, which facilitates the understanding and communication of complicated information.

You can obtain deeper insights into your target market, collect data more effectively, and streamline your market research process by utilizing technology.

In summary

One of the most important phases in the product development process is conducting market research. Making educated selections regarding your product is made possible by the insightful information it offers about your target market, consumer demands, and market demand. Utilizing technology and a combination of primary and secondary research methodologies, you can collect precise and insightful data to inform your strategy for developing new products. Keep in mind that conducting market research is a continuous activity that needs to be reviewed frequently to keep up with shifting consumer preferences and market dynamics.

7.3 Creating a Product Design and Prototype

The next critical stage in the product development process is designing and prototyping your product, which comes after you have carried out in-depth market research and determined which product idea is feasible. To make sure your product fulfills the demands and expectations of your target market, design and prototyping are crucial. We will go over the main ideas and procedures for creating and prototyping your product in this section.

7.3.1 Specifying the Needs for the Product

It's crucial to specify your product's specifications precisely before starting the design and development process. This entails knowing what attributes, capabilities, and characteristics your product should have in order to satisfy the demands of your intended market. Use focus groups, interviews, and user surveys to get insightful information and input from prospective clients. This will assist you in determining which important features and functionalities to put first in your product.

When determining your product's needs, it's also critical to take into account aspects like cost, manufacturing feasibility, and regulatory constraints. By striking a balance between these variables, you can make sure that your product is feasible to create, complies with applicable laws, and is appealing to consumers.

7.3.2 Developing the Design Concept

After you have a firm grasp on the specifications for your product, it's time to start thinking through the design. This entails converting the specifications for your product into a picture that effectively conveys its features. To realize your concept, think about collaborating with an experienced industrial designer or design team.

It's critical to concentrate on developing a design that is not only aesthetically beautiful but also practical and user-friendly at the conceptualization stage. Think about your product's usability, ergonomics, and general user experience. Iteratively improve the design in response to input from industry experts and prospective clients.

7.3.3 Formulating Detailed Specifications for Products

After developing a strong design concept, it's critical to draft comprehensive product specifications. These specs include your product's dimensions, materials, components, and production procedures, along with other technical information and needs. In-depth product requirements are essential for productive interactions with suppliers and manufacturers.

In order to guarantee that the product specs are precise and practical, think about collaborating closely with engineers and technical specialists. Work together with suppliers and manufacturers to comprehend their capacities and constraints so that you can modify the standards as needed.

7.3.4 Constructing a Prototype

Now that you have the product specifications,

it's time to create a prototype. A prototype is a functional model or representation of your product that lets you assess and gauge its overall performance, usability, and functionality. In order to hone and enhance a product's design, several iterations of the product are made during the prototyping phase.

Prototyping can be done in a number of ways, from straightforward handcrafted prototypes to sophisticated computer-aided design (CAD) models and 3D printing. The complexity of your project, the resources you have at your disposal, and your budget all play a role in the prototyping approach you choose.

It's critical to get input from stakeholders, specialists, and possible customers throughout the prototyping stage. You can use this input to pinpoint any areas that need improvement or design problems. Rework the design in light of the comments you've received, and make new prototypes as needed.

7.3.5 Verifying and Experimenting with the Model Testing and validating a prototype's performance in depth is essential after it has been developed. To test if the prototype performs as anticipated, it is put through a variety of scenarios and conditions. This entails evaluating its robustness, dependability, and harmony with other parts or systems.

To get input on the prototype's usability and user experience, think about holding user testing sessions. This will assist you in determining any usability problems or potential improvement areas. It's also a good idea to consult with industry professionals to confirm the prototype's technical specifications.

Make the required changes and improvements to the design in light of the feedback and test results. Work on the prototype iteratively until you are satisfied that it fulfills the necessary requirements and functions as intended.

7.3.6 Concluding the Design

It's time to complete the design when the prototype has been successfully tested and validated. This entails applying any modifications or enhancements that are required in light of the input gathered during the testing stage. Assist your design team and technical specialists in close collaboration to guarantee that the final design satisfies all necessary requirements and is optimized for manufacturing.

Cost optimization, manufacturability, and scalability are critical considerations throughout the finalization stage. Work together with suppliers and manufacturers to make sure the design can be manufactured at scale effectively and with minimal loss of quality.

7.3.7 Recording the Architecture

It is essential to record all design specifications, technical drawings, and other pertinent data as you bring the design to completion. Future revisions of the product, production, and quality control can all refer to this documentation. It also makes communication with suppliers and manufacturers easier and contributes to the protection of your intellectual property.

To make sure that your design is appropriately safeguarded by patents or other types of intellectual property rights, think about collaborating with a patent attorney or intellectual property specialist.

7.3.8 Synopsis

One of the most important phases in the product development process is designing and prototyping your product. With its help, you may turn your concept for a product into a working, actual prototype that can be tried and tested. The procedures described in this section will enable you to develop a well-thought-out and optimized product that satisfies the requirements and demands of your intended market. To guarantee that your finished product is of the highest caliber, never forget to iterate and improve your design in response to comments and testing outcomes.

7.4 Evaluate and refine your product

Testing and iterating are vital steps in the product development process that come after designing and prototyping your idea. Testing gives you the chance to get user input and assess the functionality, usability, and performance of your product. Iterating entails adjusting and improving your product in response to feedback, making sure that it fulfills the requirements and expectations of your intended market. We will discuss the value of testing and iterating your product in this section and show you some useful tips on how to do it efficiently.

7.4.1 The Value of Examination

There are a number of reasons why testing your product is crucial. First of all, it enables you to locate any defects or problems that might be present in your goods. Early detection of these issues allows you to address them before your product is released onto the market, saving you money, time, and sometimes even reputational harm. Testing also assists you in making sure that your product functions as intended and satisfies the necessary quality requirements.

Second, testing offers insightful information about how your intended customer base views and uses your product. By obtaining input from prospective clients, you can learn more about their requirements, inclinations, and problems. You may improve your product and make it more enticing and user-friendly by using this knowledge.

Finally, testing enables you to verify your product-related assumptions and hypotheses. It assists you in ascertaining whether your product adds value to your target market and resolves the issue it was intended to address. You can get proof for your statements and make data-driven choices by putting your product through real user testing.

7.4.2 Test Types

You can test different components of your product in different ways to assess different aspects of it. The following are a few typical test types:

Testing for usability

The goal of usability testing is to determine how simple and intuitive your product is for users to use. It entails watching people as they use your product to complete particular activities and gathering feedback on their experience. You can find any usability problems, such as ambiguous directions, challenging-to-use features, or confusing navigation, by doing usability testing. You can improve the general user experience and raise customer satisfaction by taking care of these problems.

Testing for functionality

Functionality testing evaluates how well and consistently your product carries out its intended functions. It entails putting your product through its paces to make sure that every feature and component functions as it should. Functionality testing aids in finding any errors, hiccups, or malfunctions that can impair your product's functionality. You may improve your product's dependability and functionality by resolving these problems.

Execution Evaluation

The goal of performance testing is to determine how well your product functions under various loads and circumstances. It entails evaluating your product's speed, responsiveness, and stability to make sure it can manage the anticipated workload. You can find any scalability problems or performance bottlenecks that could affect the user experience by conducting performance testing. Your clients can have a smooth and satisfying experience if you optimize the performance of your product.

Comparative Evaluation

A/B testing, sometimes referred to as split testing, compares two or more iterations of your product to see which one works better. It enables you to test several iterations of your product—such as altered features, designs, or price points— and assess how they affect the preferences and behavior of users. Utilizing A/B testing enables you to optimize your product according to consumer demand and user preferences while making data-driven decisions.

7.4.3 Techniques for Testing and Iteration That Work

Think about implementing the following tactics to make sure your testing and iteration process is successful:

Establish specific testing objectives.
Make sure your testing objectives are well-defined before you start any tests. Which particular features of your product are you looking to assess? Which inquiries are you seeking answers for? You may concentrate your testing efforts and obtain pertinent and useful feedback by establishing defined objectives.

Determine Who Your Target Market Is
Determine who your testing target audience is. Who are the possible customers for your offering? Which behaviors, tastes, or demographics should we take into account? You can obtain input that is more pertinent and representative of your real user base by choosing a sample that is typical of your target market.

Construct practical testing circumstances.
Make sure the testing scenarios you create closely mimic actual user interactions with your product. You'll be able to get more precise comments and

insights as a result. When developing testing scenarios, take into account elements like context, environment, and user goals.

Get both qualitative and quantitative information. While you are testing, collect both quantitative and qualitative data. Metrics and analytics, two types of quantitative data, can offer unbiased perceptions of user behavior and product performance. User comments and observations, for example, are examples of qualitative data that can offer subjective insights into user preferences, problems, and suggestions for change.

Rework Depending on Feedback
Once the input has been gathered, evaluate the information and pinpoint areas that need work. Sort the input according to importance and viability, then create an iterative plan to fix the problems that you find. After making the required adjustments and alterations to your product, carry out additional testing to confirm the success of the enhancements.

Constantly evaluate and improve
Throughout the entire process of developing a product, testing and iteration should be continuous activities. To make sure you are headed in the right direction as you make improvements and modifications to your product, keep testing and getting user feedback. Adopt a culture of constant adaptation and improvement to keep ahead of the competition and satisfy the changing

demands of your target market.

You may successfully test and iterate your product using these techniques, making sure it fulfills the needs of your target market and differentiates itself in a crowded industry. Iteration and testing are crucial steps in the product development process that help you produce a high-caliber, user-friendly, and ready-for-market product.

MANAGING FINANCES AND OPERATIONS

8.1 Formulating a Budget and Financial Plan

The development of a sound financial strategy and budget is one of the most important components of running a business. A budget aids in the efficient use of resources and the making of well-informed decisions, while a financial plan acts as a guide for the financial stability and success of your company. We will go over the main procedures for drafting a budget and financial plan for your company in this part.

8.1.1 Determining Your Needs for Money

Evaluating your company's financial needs is crucial before getting into the specifics of making a budget and financial plan. Determine how much money you'll need to start and run your firm first. Take into account elements like tools, stock, advertising expenditures, wages, and overhead. To guarantee that your estimation of your financial needs is accurate, carry out in-depth research and speak with professionals in the field.

Additionally, assess the cash flow needs of your company. Any business depends on cash flow, so knowing what your needs are in this area will help you prepare for any future surpluses or shortfalls. Examine your anticipated revenue and outlays to determine when your cash flow will be at its highest and lowest. You'll be able to properly manage your finances by using the information from this study to guide your decisions.

8.1.2 Formulating an Economic Projection

It's time to make a financial projection after you have evaluated your financial requirements. A financial forecast is an estimate of the future financial performance of your company made using past data and conjecture. Balance sheets, cash flow statements, and anticipated income statements are usually included.

Estimate your revenue expectations first. Take into account elements like sales volume, price strategy, and market demand. When making estimates, be cautious and reasonable while accounting for probable difficulties and unknowns.

Next, list the costs you expect to incur. Sort them into two categories: variable costs (such as raw materials and marketing charges) and fixed costs (like rent and utilities). To make sure that your spending estimates are realistic and correct, look up industry benchmarks and speak with industry professionals.

Projected financial statements can be made once your revenue and expenses have been predicted. These financial statements will give you a quick overview of your company's financial situation for a given time frame, usually one to three years. To produce precise and thorough financial estimates, use financial modeling software or speak with a financial expert.

8.1.3 Budget Development

Now that you have a financial projection, it's time to create a budget. A budget is a thorough strategy that specifies how you will use your money to reach your company's objectives. It assists you in keeping tabs on and managing your expenditure, spotting areas where you're overpaying or underspending, and making the required corrections.

To begin, group your spending into various budget categories, including overhead, marketing, operations, and salary. Determine a precise monetary value for every category by considering your business priorities and budgetary projections. A suitable amount of money should be set aside for necessities like marketing and research and development.

When creating your budget, think about including a contingency reserve to cover unforeseen costs or emergencies. It's usually a good idea to plan ahead for unanticipated events that can occur when running your business.

8.1.4 Keeping an eye on and evaluating your budget and financial plan

Making a budget and financial plan is a continuous process. To make sure it remains relevant and successful, it needs to be continuously reviewed and monitored. Monitor your real financial performance on a regular basis in comparison to your budget and expected financial statements.

Look for any differences between your projected and actual revenue and expenses. Examine the causes of these differences and modify your budget and financial strategy as needed. By going through this procedure, you'll be able to pinpoint your areas for growth and make wise choices that will maximize your financial performance.

Furthermore, make sure your budget is in line with your company's aims and goals by reviewing it on a regular basis. Your financial requirements could vary as your company grows. Be ready to make necessary revisions and updates to your budget and financial plan.

8.1.5 Getting Expert Counsel

It might be difficult to create a financial plan and budget if you are unfamiliar with financial ideas and procedures. Think about consulting a financial advisor or accountant that specializes in working with small businesses for expert help. They can offer insightful advice, guide you through tricky financial situations, and guarantee the accuracy and efficiency of your budget and financial plan.

Recall that having a well-designed budget and financial plan are crucial for efficiently managing the money of your company. You will be well-equipped to make wise financial decisions and guide your company toward success if you evaluate your needs, produce a financial forecast, create a budget, and routinely monitor and analyze your financial plan.

8.2 Handling Expenses and Cash Flow

Keeping an eye on spending and cash flow is one of the most important parts of operating a successful business. The movement of money into and out of your company is referred to as cash flow, whereas expenses are all of the costs involved in maintaining your organization. It is imperative that you manage these two elements well if you want your firm to be sustainable and financially sound.

8.2.1 Comprehending Cash Flow

Monitoring and managing your company's cash intake and outflow is known as cash flow management. Understanding your cash flow clearly is essential to making sure you have the money to pay for your bills and fulfill your financial commitments.

Revenue from sales, investments, loans, and any other sources of money for your company are all considered cash inflows. To make sure you have a consistent flow of money to support your operations, it's critical to precisely track and forecast your cash inflows.

In order to efficiently handle your incoming cash, take into account the following tactics:

Promptly send invoices: To guarantee on-time payment, send out invoices to your clients as soon as feasible. Establish a method for monitoring and pursuing unpaid invoices.

Provide discounts or other incentives to encourage early payments from your clients. This will encourage them to pay their invoices on time. By hastening the recovery of receivables, this can enhance your cash flow.

It's a good idea to diversify your sources of income because depending just on one can be dangerous. Examine ways to offer supplementary goods or services that enhance your main line of business in order to diversify your sources of income.

Money Disbursements
The costs associated with operating your business, including rent, payroll, utilities, inventory, and other operating expenses, are referred to as cash outflows. Effective cash outflow management is essential if you want to prevent overspending and make sure you have enough money to pay your bills.

In order to effectively manage your financial withdrawals, take into account the following tactics:

Establish a budget. Create a detailed budget that details the costs you anticipate incurring during each period. Review and revise your budget on a regular basis to account for modifications to your company's activities.

Develop a solid rapport with your suppliers and work out advantageous conditions for payments. To cut expenses, look into opportunities for bulk purchases or ask for discounts for early payment.

Reduce discretionary spending: Find places where you can cut costs without sacrificing the caliber of your goods or services. Put in place cost-cutting strategies like remote work opportunities or energy-efficient procedures.

8.2.2 Forecasting cash flow
Using past data and predicted changes to your company's operations, cash flow forecasting entails estimating your future cash inflows and outflows. It facilitates the anticipation of prospective cash surpluses or shortages and empowers you to make well-informed decisions for efficient cash flow management.

Procedures for Forecasting Cash Flow
Compile historical information. To spot patterns and trends, gather and examine your previous cash flow statements. Your cash flow prediction will be built around this data.

Determine the main drivers: Identify the variables that affect your cash flow, such as market trends, seasonality, or adjustments to the way your company operates. Take into account all potential external and internal influences on your cash flow.

Project future cash inflows: Make an estimate of your future cash inflows using your market analysis and previous data. Take into account variables including expected sales, terms of payment, and collection times.

Project future cash outflows: Make a projection of your costs based on past expenditure trends and any expected adjustments to your company's operations. Add all one-time charges, variable costs, and fixed costs.

Examine the prediction: To find any possible cash surpluses or shortfalls, compare your anticipated cash inflows and outflows. You may manage your cash flow more efficiently by taking proactive steps and making well-informed decisions, with the support of our study.

Update and monitor: Continually compare your projected cash flow to your actual cash flow. As your company's activities or the state of the market change, update your forecast accordingly.

8.2.3 Taking Care of Bills

In order to maximize profitability and preserve a healthy cash flow, spending management is essential. You can maximize your resources and direct money toward areas that yield the best return on investment by keeping a close eye on your spending.

Expense management techniques
Set spending priorities. Sort your spending into categories that are necessary and non-essential. To free up resources for important aspects of your organization, concentrate on cutting or getting rid of non-essential spending.

Engage in vendor negotiations: Examine your vendor agreements on a regular basis and work out better terms or price breaks. To cut expenses, look at opportunities for bulk purchases or other providers.

Put cost-cutting initiatives into action: Determine where you can cut costs without sacrificing the caliber of your goods or services. This could involve measures to reduce waste, streamline your supply chain, or adopt energy-efficient methods.

Leverage technology: Use technology to automate procedures and cut expenses associated with manual labor. Use digital solutions, such as project management platforms, inventory management tools, and accounting systems, to optimize your business processes.

Evaluate expenditure frequently: To find areas of excessive spending or inefficiency, evaluate spending frequently. Examine your spending and search for areas where you may save money.

In summary

An essential component of managing a successful business is controlling spending and cash flow. You can make sure your business is financially sound and sustainable by knowing current cash flow, projecting future cash flows, and controlling your spending well. By putting good cash flow management techniques into place, you'll be able to manage your finances, distribute resources wisely, and overcome any unforeseen obstacles.

8.3 Putting in Place Efficient Operational Procedures

Setting up efficient operational procedures is essential for ensuring seamless daily operations as soon as your organization is up and running. The actions and protocols required to create and provide your goods and services are included in your operational processes. You may increase customer happiness, cut expenses, and boost production by putting in place effective operational procedures. This part will cover the essential procedures for putting into place efficient operational processes and offer helpful advice on how to improve the efficiency of your company's operations.

8.3.1 Organizing Your Workflow

It's critical to comprehend how your operational processes are currently operating before making any improvements. To find any bottlenecks or inefficiencies, begin by carefully outlining your current operations. You will be able to see the dependencies, possible areas for improvement, and the flow of tasks with the aid of this process mapping exercise. Think about including your teammates in this task as well; they can offer insightful comments and suggestions for improvement.

8.3.2 Finding Opportunities for Development
After you have your processes drawn out, it's time to find areas for improvement. Seek out any steps that are prone to mistakes, delays, bottlenecks, or redundancies. To obtain a comprehensive understanding of the problems with your operational procedures, take into account the input from both your clients and your team. With the aid of this study, you may allocate resources appropriately and prioritize the areas that need immediate attention.

8.3.3 Simplifying the Process
Optimizing your work process is essential for raising operational effectiveness. Seek to streamline processes, automate tedious work, and allocate resources as efficiently as possible. For instance, you can use technological solutions to automate labor-intensive tasks like order processing and inventory management. Streamlining your workflow can help you save time, cut down on errors, and use resources more wisely.

8.3.4 Standard Operating Procedures
In order to maintain consistency and quality

in your operations, standardizing procedures is crucial. Standard operating procedures (SOPs) that provide detailed instructions should be created and should include documentation of the best practices for each process. SOPs help to preserve uniformity even in the event of staff changes by acting as a reference manual for your team members. Review and update your SOPs frequently to reflect any modifications to industry regulations or process enhancements.

8.3.5 Education and Training

Invest in team-member training and development initiatives to guarantee that your operational procedures are carried out efficiently. Give them the abilities and information they need to complete their jobs quickly and effectively. Technical skills like utilizing software or managing machines can be included in training, as can soft skills like problem-solving and communication. Evaluate your team's training needs on a regular basis and give them opportunities for continued development to help them become more capable.

8.3.6 Ongoing Enhancement

It is important to see operational procedures as dynamic and always improving. Promote a culture of continuous improvement in your company, giving team members the freedom to find and recommend ways to improve processes. Review your procedures on a regular basis, get input from your staff and clients, and make necessary adjustments. Adopting a continual improvement approach can help you stay ahead of the competition and adjust to changing consumer needs.

8.3.7 Observation and Assessment

Set up key performance indicators (KPIs) and periodically assess their performance to make sure your operational processes are effective. Metrics like customer satisfaction, production output, and process cycle time are examples of KPIs. Employ data analytics tools to collect and examine pertinent data so that you can notice patterns, pinpoint areas in need of development, and make decisions based on facts. To meet your business objectives, evaluate your KPIs on a regular basis and make necessary adjustments to your operating procedures.

8.3.8 Cooperation and Interaction

Collaboration and communication are essential to the success of operational procedures. Encourage an environment in which team members feel free to voice their problems, ideas, and suggestions for change. To dismantle organizational silos and advance a comprehensive comprehension of the operational procedures, foster cross-functional cooperation. To promote communication and make sure that everyone is on the same page and working toward the same objectives, make use of collaborative tools and platforms.

8.3.9 Handling of Risks

Risks and difficulties are not unaffected by operational procedures. Establish a strong framework for risk management to help you recognize, evaluate, and reduce any risks that could affect your business operations. Evaluate your procedures on a regular basis to find any weaknesses and create backup strategies to reduce interruptions. You can guarantee the continuation of your business operations and uphold client satisfaction by taking proactive risk management measures.

8.3.10 Automation and Outsourcing

To further optimize your operational operations, think about using automation technology or outsourcing non-core tasks. You can save money and gain specialized knowledge by outsourcing while concentrating on your main skills. Artificial intelligence (AI) and robotic process automation (RPA) are two examples of automation technologies that can increase productivity by streamlining repetitive operations. Based on your company's needs, weigh the possible advantages and disadvantages of outsourcing and automation and make wise judgments.

Establishing efficient operational procedures is essential to your company's long-term success. You may increase operational efficiency and spur business growth by mapping your processes, finding areas for improvement, optimizing workflows, standardizing procedures, and funding training and development. Adopt a culture of constant improvement, track and assess performance, encourage cooperation and dialogue, and take proactive risk management measures. You can make sure that your operational procedures are optimized to meet your business objectives and provide outstanding value to your clients by putting these tactics into practice.

8.4 Tracking and Examining Important Financial Data

After starting out, it's critical to track and evaluate important financial data to make sure your company stays successful. Financial metrics give you important information about the performance and health of your company's finances, empowering you to take proactive steps and make wise decisions to promote growth and profitability. This section will address some of the most crucial financial indicators that any entrepreneur should be tracking, as well as the significance of tracking and evaluating these metrics.

8.4.1 Realizing the Significance of Financial

Measures

Financial indicators are a good way to gauge how well your company is doing overall. You may have a better grasp of your company's financial situation, pinpoint its strengths and weaknesses, and make data-driven decisions to streamline operations by monitoring and evaluating these measures. The following are some major arguments for the necessity of tracking financial metrics:

1. Evaluating Financial Health: Financial indicators give you an overview of the health of your company's finances, enabling you to assess its solvency, profitability, and liquidity. You can discover any possible financial risks or difficulties and take appropriate measures to mitigate them by routinely analyzing these metrics.

2. Performance Evaluation: You can evaluate your company's performance in relation to your goals and objectives by using financial measures. Through a comparison of actual outcomes with your financial forecasts and benchmarks, you may determine what aspects of your organization are performing well and what still needs work.

3. Finding Trends and Patterns: Analyzing financial data over an extended period of time enables you to spot patterns and trends in the financial performance of your company. With this knowledge, you may proactively modify your operations and strategy to take advantage of

future possibilities or problems.

4. Communication with Investors and Stakeholders: Financial indicators are essential for informing investors, lenders, and other stakeholders about your company's financial performance. You may draw in possible partners or investors and increase trust and confidence in your company by providing accurate and current financial information.

8.4.2 Crucial Financial KPIs to Track

You can monitor a wide range of financial measures, but it's critical to concentrate on the ones that are most pertinent to your company and sector. The following crucial financial indicators are worth keeping an eye on for any entrepreneur:

1. Revenue: The total amount of money your company makes from its core operations is known as revenue. Monitoring your revenue enables you to assess the success of your marketing and sales initiatives as well as gauge the expansion of your company over time.

2. Gross Profit Margin: The amount of income left over after subtracting the direct costs of creating or providing your good or service is known as the gross profit margin. Keeping an eye on your gross profit margin enables you to evaluate how well your pricing and operations are working.

3. Net Profit Margin: The amount of income left over after all costs, such as interest, taxes, and operational costs, have been subtracted is known

as the net profit margin. This measure sheds light on the overall profitability and long-term profitability of your company.

4. Cash Flow: Over a given time period, cash flow tracks the flow of money into and out of your company. It's critical to keep an eye on your cash flow to make sure you have the resources necessary to fulfill your debt repayment commitments to creditors, suppliers, and staff.

5. Accounts Receivable Turnover: This indicator shows how rapidly your company receives payments from clients. While a low ratio could point to possible problems with credit management or customer payment delays, a high turnover ratio shows that your company is effective at collecting payments.

6. Inventory Turnover: This is a gauge of how rapidly your company sells its stock. By keeping an eye on this indicator, you can enhance cash flow, prevent stockouts and overstocking, and manage your inventory more effectively.

7. Return on Investment (ROI): ROI calculates how much money an investment returns in comparison to how much it costs. You can evaluate the efficacy of various business components, such as capital investments or marketing initiatives, and make well-informed judgments regarding resource allocation by computing the return on investment (ROI).

8.4.3 Financial Analysis Instruments and Methodologies

It's critical to use the right tools and methods in order to track and evaluate your financial indicators. Here are a few methods and instruments for financial analysis that are frequently used:

1. Financial Statements: A thorough picture of your company's financial performance is provided by financial statements, including the income statement, balance sheet, and cash flow statement. You can find trends, patterns, and areas that need attention by routinely going over these assertions.

2. Ratio Analysis: To evaluate the financial performance and well-being of your company, ratio analysis entails computing and analyzing a variety of financial ratios. Liquidity, profitability, and efficiency ratios are examples of common ratios. You can obtain insights into the relative performance of your organization by contrasting these ratios with industry standards or historical data.

3. Budgeting and Forecasting: You can compare actual outcomes with your estimates by creating a thorough budget and revising your financial forecasts on a regular basis. This assists you in spotting any deviations and implementing the necessary adjustments to keep your company operating as planned.

4. Financial Software: Tracking and analyzing financial indicators can be made more efficient by

using accounting systems or financial software. These technologies produce reports, automate computations, and give you real-time access to the financial health of your company.

In summary

Your company's long-term success depends on your ability to track and evaluate important financial data. Through comprehending the significance of financial metrics, monitoring crucial metrics, and utilizing suitable tools and methodologies, you can arrive at well-informed selections, pinpoint opportunities for enhancement, and stimulate expansion and financial gain. Recall that financial indicators convey more than just numbers; they also tell the tale of the success and health of your company's finances. You may achieve your entrepreneurial goals and confidently navigate the financial landscape by routinely evaluating and analyzing these KPIs.

SCALING YOUR BUSINESS

9.1 Formulating a Strategy for Scalability

A business's ability to scale is essential to its

development and success. It entails reaching new markets, growing revenue, and expanding operations. To achieve sustainable growth, scaling a firm involves meticulous planning and execution. We'll go over the essential components of creating a scaling plan in this section, which will help your company expand and succeed.

9.1.1 Evaluating the Scalability Potential of Your Company

It is crucial to evaluate the scalability potential of your firm before beginning the process of scaling it. Not every firm can grow to the same extent, so knowing the opportunities and constraints specific to your industry will help you make wise choices. Here are some things to think about when determining how scalable your company is:

Market Requirements

Analyze the market's demand for your good or service. Does your company have a sizable and expanding consumer base that could help it grow? To determine possible areas for expansion and to determine the size of your target market, conduct market research.

Efficiency of Operations

Evaluate how well your present activities are working. Are you streamlining and optimizing your processes? Growing a company with inefficient operations might result in higher expenses and lower client satisfaction. Determine areas that require improvement and put plans into action to boost operational effectiveness.

Modular Business Plan

Check to see if your business model is naturally scalable. Because they are digital in nature, some business models, like software-as-a-service (SaaS) and e-commerce, are naturally scalable. Look at ways to change or adjust your business model if it's not naturally scalable in order to support expansion.

Resources Accessible

Think about the tools at your disposal to assist in the expansion of your company. This covers collaborations, financial resources, human capital, and technological infrastructure. Determine whether you have the resources you need to scale successfully or if you need to find more money or form strategic partnerships.

9.1.2 Clearly Determining Growth Goals

Having determined the potential scalability of your company, it is critical to establish specific growth goals. These goals will act as a guide for your scaling plan and a standard by which to evaluate its accomplishment. The following are essential actions for establishing growth goals:

Describe your goals.

Establish your long-term goals for the company first. What goals do you have for the ensuing five or ten years? Your growth ambitions and ability to maintain focus on your end goals will be guided by this vision.

Determine the KPIs, or key performance indicators.
Determine the important measures that will show the expansion and success of your company. Revenue goals, market share, customer acquisition rates, and any other pertinent data unique to your industry can be included in these KPIs. You can monitor your progress and make data-driven decisions by setting quantifiable KPIs.

Divide your goals into milestones.
Divide your growth goals into more manageable, smaller goals. As a result, scaling will be easier to handle, giving you a sense of success as you go. Every milestone ought to have a precise timeframe and a set of steps that must be taken to reach it.

Match resources to objectives.
Make sure your growth goals are in line with the resources your company has at its disposal. Overscaling in the absence of sufficient resources can result in subpar quality and inefficiencies in operations. Take into account the technological, human, and financial resources needed to accomplish each goal.

9.1.3 Reaching a Wider Audience
Entering new markets is a typical corporate scaling tactic. It enables you to diversify your revenue sources and reach new client segments. The following actions are something to think

about while reaching a wider audience:

Market Analysis

To find possible new markets for your good or service, do extensive market research. Examine consumer inclinations, market developments, and rivalry in each intended market. You can use this research to ascertain whether there is a market for your item in various areas or among particular demographics.

Modify your product or service.

Adapt your offering to the unique requirements and inclinations of the target market. This could entail changing your features, branding, price, or packaging. Your chances of success in new areas will rise if you modify your offering to meet the needs of the local market.

Create channels of distribution.

Create efficient distribution channels to connect with consumers in the upcoming market. This could entail creating online sales platforms, establishing physical stores, or collaborating with regional distributors. Think about the best and most affordable ways to market and distribute your goods or services in each of your target markets.

Orient marketing and sales practices locally.

Modify your sales and marketing tactics to appeal to the target audience. This entails modifying advertising campaigns, translating marketing materials, and utilizing regional media outlets or influencers. By localizing your marketing, you may establish a stronger relationship with consumers and increase brand recognition in the target market.

9.1.4 Making the Most of Strategic Alliances

Forming strategic alliances can be very helpful in growing your company. Working together with other companies or groups will give you access to new markets, resources, and knowledge. Here are a few strategies for utilizing strategic alliances:

Determine Possible Partners
Determine which companies or groups fit in with your offerings or have a comparable target market. Seek out chances to work together on cooperative product development, marketing initiatives, or distribution networks. Take into account companies that can benefit your clients in addition to those who are direct competitors.

Make arrangements that will benefit both parties. When reaching out to possible partners, concentrate on drafting agreements that will benefit both parties. Clearly state the partnership's value proposition for each party and how it will help them achieve their own growth goals. To guarantee that a collaboration is effective, lay out the terms and expectations clearly.

Utilize current networks.
Use business networks, trade groups, and your

current network of contacts to find possible joint ventures. Attend trade fairs, conferences, or industry events to network with other like-minded business owners and discuss potential joint ventures.

Keep an eye on and assess partnerships

Keep an eye on and assess your strategic alliances' performance on a regular basis. Evaluate whether the collaboration is helping you achieve your scalability goals and bringing about the anticipated advantages. Remain flexible when modifying or ending relationships that don't support your company's goals.

In summary

Creating a scaling strategy is crucial for companies that want to expand and succeed. You may position your company for sustained expansion by determining its scalability potential, establishing specific growth goals, reaching a wider audience, and utilizing strategic alliances. Keep in mind that achieving scalability is an ongoing effort that calls for flexibility and an openness to change. To guarantee long-term success, remain flexible, keep an eye on market developments, and be ready to modify your plan of action as necessary.

9.2 Developing New Markets

A key component of your company's development and success is market expansion. It enables you to expand your clientele, generate more income, and diversify your line of work. But breaking into new markets can be difficult and requires thorough preparation and execution. We will look at the tactics and factors to take into account while growing your company into new markets in this part.

9.2.1 Analysis and Research on the Market

Doing in-depth market research and analysis is crucial before entering new markets. This will assist you in determining prospective business prospects, comprehending the competitive environment, and evaluating the level of demand in the new market for your goods or services. Take into consideration these crucial steps:

Determine your target markets: Choose the markets that have the potential to expand and fit in with your company's objectives. Take into account variables including regulations, cultural differences, economic situations, and demographics.

Examine competitors: Find out about and evaluate your rivals in the new market. Determine their market share, advantages, and disadvantages. This will assist you in formulating plans to set your company apart from the competition and obtain a competitive edge.

Analyze market demand: Determine whether there is a need in the new market for your goods or services. To learn more about potential customers, hold focus groups, interviews, and surveys. This will assist you in customizing your services to suit their tastes and demands.

Assess the obstacles to market entry: Determine any obstacles to entry, such as rules and regulations, cultural or linguistic hurdles, established rivals, or legal restrictions. Create plans to get through these obstacles and guarantee a seamless market debut.

9.2.2 Creating a Plan for Entering the Market
It's time to create a market entry plan when you've finished your market analysis and research. This plan will specify how you want to join the new market and build your brand there. Here are some crucial things to remember:

Select the best entry strategy: There are a number

of strategies to take into account, including joint ventures, exporting, licensing, franchising, exporting, and establishing a subsidiary. Every mode has benefits and drawbacks. Determine which mode best fits your needs in terms of resources, capabilities, and business goals.

Modify your goods or offerings: Make sure your goods and services are customized to the unique requirements and tastes of the target market. Take into account elements like localization, branding, packaging, and price. To make sure your products or services are appealing to the intended audience, test the market and receive feedback.

Create distribution channels. Determine which distribution methods will help you efficiently reach your target audience. This can entail establishing your own physical stores or offices, partnering with regional distributors, or using e-commerce platforms.

Create local alliances: Work together with regional partners to take advantage of their networks, resources, and expertise. Examples of these partners include suppliers, distributors, and strategic alliances. You may better negotiate cultural quirks, comply with legal obligations, and obtain market insights by cultivating strong partnerships with regional partners.

9.2.3 Promotion and Marketing in Emerging Markets

A customized marketing and promotional plan is necessary when entering new markets in order to connect and interact with your target audience. Here are some crucial things to remember:

Recognize cultural quirks: Make sure that your branding, communication tactics, and marketing messaging are appropriate for the local way of life. Take into account elements like language, customs, values, and customer behavior.

Adapt your marketing collateral to the local market. Localize and translate your marketing materials, such as product packaging, social media posts, websites, and ads. Make sure the messaging you use is pertinent to the target market and respectful of cultural differences.

Make use of digital marketing channels to connect with your target market in the new area. Search engine optimization (SEO), content marketing, influencer relationships, and social media marketing are a few examples of this. Adapt your digital marketing tactics to the target market's interests and particular platforms.

Interact with the community: To establish credibility and trust, cultivate relationships with local authorities and communities. Take part in regional gatherings, provide funding for regional projects, and work with regional influencers or groups to create talk about your business.

9.2.4 Handling Difficulties and Risks

Entering new markets carries a certain amount of risk and difficulty. It's critical to be organized and have backup plans ready. Here are some crucial things to remember:

Legal and regulatory compliance: Become acquainted with the new market's legal and regulatory requirements. Make sure you abide by all applicable licenses, permits, tax requirements, and employment rules. Consult a lawyer if necessary.

Financial considerations: Increase the amount of money you budget for in order to cover the expenses of entering a new market. Take into account variables such as the cost of entering a new market, marketing expenditures, operating costs, and possible currency fluctuations. Make sure you have enough cash on hand to fund your plans for growth.

Language and cultural obstacles: Be ready to overcome these obstacles. Invest in cultural training for your staff, seek out local talent with market knowledge, and set up efficient routes of communication to overcome any language barriers.

Monitor and adjust: Keep a close eye on your success in the new market and make adjustments as needed. Customer feedback should be gathered, KPIs should be monitored, and any necessary strategy revisions should be made. Remain flexible and open to adjusting to shifting consumer demands and market conditions.

Entering new markets can be a game-changer for your company. You may prepare your company for success in new markets by carrying out in-depth market research, creating a market entry strategy, adjusting your marketing efforts, and efficiently managing risks. Accept the chances and difficulties that come with growth, but don't lose sight of your long-term objectives.

9.3 Establishing Strategic Alliances

Developing strategic alliances is essential to growing your company and succeeding in the long run. You can increase your growth and reach by making partnerships with other companies or organizations and taking advantage of their networks, resources, and experience. Forming strategic alliances can expand your product options, provide you access to new markets, draw in new clients, and raise awareness of your brand. The main actions and factors to be taken into account when forming strategic alliances will be discussed in this section.

9.3.1 Finding Possible Affiliates

Finding possible partners that share your values and business goals is the first stage in creating strategic alliances. Seek out businesses or associations that have skills in fields that can help your company, target customers who are comparable to yours, or compliment your offerings in terms of goods or services. Take into account businesses in allied industries that may present synergistic potential as well as direct competitors.

Analyze your industry landscape and carry out in-depth market research to find possible partners. Seek out businesses with a solid track record, comparable development direction, and a solid reputation. Attend trade exhibits, conferences, and networking gatherings to meet possible business partners and gain insight into their operations. Additionally, investigate possible collaboration options by utilizing professional networks and internet platforms.

9.3.2 Assessing Prospects for Collaboration
It's critical to assess partnership chances after you've discovered possible partners to make sure they support your company's goals. When assessing potential partnerships, take into account the following factors:

Analyze the partnership's strategic fit in relation to your long-term objectives and business plan. Determine whether the collaboration will enable you to meet your goals, including growing into new markets, gaining access to new clients, or improving your line of products.

Complementary Resources: Find out what resources the possible collaborator is able to provide. This can include access to a particular market niche, financial resources, technology, knowledge, and distribution methods. Examine the ways in which these resources can enhance your current skills and further your development.

Reputation and Values: Consider the business culture, values, and reputation of the possible partner. Make sure your values and theirs coincide in order to keep your union peaceful and fruitful. Strong values and congruence can result in more fruitful and advantageous teamwork.

Compatibility: Evaluate how well the work cultures, communication philosophies, and decision-making procedures of the two firms mesh. A strong fit in these areas can reduce the likelihood of conflict and promote productive collaboration.

Risk Assessment: To identify any possible dangers or difficulties related to the relationship, carry out a comprehensive risk assessment. Take into account elements including potential conflicts of interest, legal and regulatory compliance, and financial soundness. Reduce these risks by drafting precise contracts and opening up lines of communication.

9.3.3 Making Contact with Possible Partners

It's time to reach out to possible partners when you have assessed the collaboration options and determined who would be the most qualified applicants. When reaching out to possible partners, keep the following procedures in mind:

Research and preparation: Before contacting a possible partner, thoroughly investigate their company, line of products, and most recent accomplishments. This will show that you genuinely care about the subject and enable you to adjust your strategy properly. Create a strong value proposal that emphasizes the advantages that both parties will receive from the collaboration.

Creating Contact: Use social media, phone conversations, email, and other methods to get in touch with possible partners. Be specific in your approach and state your case for why you think cooperation would be advantageous. To build rapport, point out any connections or hobbies you have in common.

First Meeting: Arrange a meeting to talk more in-depth about the collaboration if the prospective partner shows interest. Create a schedule that outlines the goals and possible advantages of the collaboration. Give them your full attention and remain receptive to their opinions.

Agreement and Negotiation: After determining

the terms and conditions of the cooperation, hold negotiations with the interested parties. This includes talking about the partnership's parameters, resource distribution, revenue sharing, intellectual property rights, and any other pertinent issues. If required, obtain legal counsel to guarantee a just and advantageous arrangement for both parties.

Formalizing the Partnership: Create a legally enforceable contract to legalize the partnership when the terms have been agreed upon. Clearly state each party's expectations as well as their duties and obligations. Provide regular avenues of communication and procedures for settling disagreements or conflicts.

9.3.4 Developing and Preserving Strategic Alliances

Developing strategic alliances is a continuous process that needs to be nurtured and maintained rather than completed in one go. The following are some essential tactics for growing and preserving your strategic alliances:

Frequent Communication: Keep lines of communication open and consistent with your partners. Arrange for check-ins or frequent meetings to talk about progress, handle any issues, and look into new prospects. Encourage a cooperative atmosphere where it is comfortable for both sides to offer suggestions and criticism.

Mutual Support: Show your partners your active support by endorsing their goods or services, introducing them to prospective clients, or offering references. Seek chances to pool resources, co-host events, or work together on collaborative marketing campaigns. You may promote mutual growth and fortify your partnership by actively helping one another.

Continuous Assessment: Keep a close eye on the partnership's effectiveness and how it is affecting your company. Keep an eye on important indicators and evaluate whether the collaboration is producing the desired outcomes. To make sure the partnership agreement stays applicable and advantageous, examine it frequently and make any required revisions.

Flexibility and Adaptability: As your businesses expand and the market conditions shift, be flexible and willing to adjust how the partnership is structured. Together, explore new avenues, tweak tactics, and adjust to developing trends. You may overcome obstacles and take advantage of fresh chances by adopting an adaptable and agile strategy.

Resolution of Conflicts: Disputes will inevitably come up in every collaboration. Provide unambiguous routes for resolving disputes, and take timely, professional action to resolve any concerns that arise. Keep lines of communication open and honest in order to settle disputes and protect the integrity of the partnership.

Developing strategic alliances can completely transform your company. You can achieve long-term success, broaden your market reach, and accelerate growth by utilizing the resources and talents of your partners. Never forget that effective communication, mutual benefit, and trust are the foundations of successful partnerships. To fully realize the potential of your partnerships and promote long-term development, cultivate and uphold them consistently.

9.4 Overcoming Growth and Scaling Difficulties
You will face a new set of chances and problems when your firm starts to grow and gain traction. Effectively managing this expansion is essential to your venture's long-term success and sustainability. This section will examine the several obstacles that arise when your business grows and offer solutions to these problems.

9.4.1 Comprehending the Process of Growth
Understanding the growth process itself is

crucial before tackling the obstacles. Increasing a company's ability to manage more clients, sales, and operations is known as scaling. This expansion can take many different forms, including diversifying product offerings, growing production capacity, and entering new markets.

It is critical to comprehend the potential for growth in your company as well as the resources needed to support that expansion. To find prospects for growth, do thorough research on your market, your rivals, and client demand. This will assist you in creating a strategy plan for efficiently managing expansion.

9.4.2 Preserving Consistency and Quality

Keeping your goods and services consistent in quality is one of the toughest tasks while your company is growing. Ensuring that every consumer receives the same level of quality and happiness gets harder as your operations grow. Poor quality might cause you to lose customers and harm your reputation.

Put your attention on creating strong quality control procedures and standards in order to overcome this obstacle. Provide your staff with frequent training opportunities to ensure consistency in the way you deliver your goods and services. Invest in automation and technology to improve efficiency and lower the possibility of mistakes or discrepancies. Gather client input on a regular basis and utilize it to streamline your operations and quickly resolve any problems.

9.4.3 Cash Flow Management

Large sums of money are needed to scale a business. You could need to spend more money on new machinery, recruit more employees, or step up your marketing as your business grows. Your cash flow may be strained by all of these operations, particularly if your revenue growth is outpacing your spending increase.

Make sure you have a thorough financial plan and budget that account for your anticipated growth in order to efficiently manage cash flow. Keep a close eye on your financial flow to spot any possible funding gaps or bottlenecks. If there are any gaps in your financial flow, think about using grants, loans, or partnerships as alternate funding sources. To guarantee that payments from clients are received on time, establish effective invoicing and payment collection procedures.

9.4.4 Growing Your Group

You'll need to scale your workforce as your company expands to accommodate higher needs. Maintaining growth requires assembling a high-performing staff and making the correct hiring decisions. But it can be difficult to attract and keep great people, particularly in a competitive job market.

Create a clear recruitment plan that supports your company's values and goals in order to overcome this obstacle. Make a detailed job description and clearly identify the jobs and duties you need to fill. Make use of online resources, industry relationships, and your network to draw in eligible applicants. Make sure the person you recruit is the ideal fit for your team by putting in place a strict interview and selection procedure.

After your team is put together, concentrate on developing a supportive and effective work environment. To support your staff in developing and adjusting to the shifting demands of the company, give them regular opportunities for training and development. To promote creativity and teamwork, cultivate an environment of open communication and cooperation.

9.4.5 Infrastructure Scaling

Your infrastructure must grow to meet the demands of your growing firm. This covers your operational procedures, technological systems, and physical space. Inadequate infrastructure can make it more difficult for you to grow and provide efficient customer service.

Examine your existing infrastructure and note any places that require modernization or enhancement. Invest in technological solutions like cloud-based platforms, inventory management software, and customer relationship management (CRM) systems that can automate and optimize your business processes. To take advantage of their resources and experience, think about partnering with outside suppliers or outsourcing some tasks.

Make sure your operating procedures are capable of handling growing volume and complexity by reviewing and improving them on a regular basis. Keep an eye on your key performance indicators (KPIs) to spot any inefficiencies or bottlenecks and take aggressive steps to fix them.

9.4.6 Adjusting to Shifts in the Market
You'll need to adjust as your company grows to reflect shifts in the market and in the industry. Your growth trajectory may be impacted by factors like competitive dynamics, technological advancements, and consumer preferences. Missed opportunities or even obsolescence may arise from a failure to adjust to these developments.

Keep up with changes in the market and new technology that may affect your sector. Keep an eye out for any changes in the tactics or products that your rivals are making. Engage with your clients on a regular basis to learn about their changing requirements and expectations.

Establish an innovative culture in your company to promote flexibility and creativity. Encourage an attitude of constant learning and development. If needed, be prepared to change your business plan or look into other markets. Accept change as a chance for personal development and maintain your flexibility when making decisions.

9.4.7 Making Use of Strategic Alliances

Establishing strategic alliances with other businesses might facilitate business scaling. Working together with leaders in the field or adjacent businesses can open up new markets and provide access to resources and knowledge.

Find possible mates who have similar ambitions and beliefs. Seek out chances to work together on joint ventures, marketing campaigns, or the co-development of goods or services. To increase your reach, take advantage of each other's networks and clientele.

Make sure that any formal agreements you enter into fully define the terms and expectations. Maintain regular communication and assess the partnership's development to make sure both parties continue to gain from it.

9.4.8 Tracking and Assessing Results

Monitoring and assessing your performance in relation to vital metrics and objectives becomes even more crucial as your firm grows. Examine your sales numbers, financial accounts, customer reviews, and other pertinent data on a regular basis to gauge your success and pinpoint areas that need work.

Establish a strong performance management system, including goal-setting, frequent performance reviews, and feedback channels. Make data-driven decisions by utilizing business intelligence and data analytics technologies to obtain insights into your operations.

Make constant iterations and refinements to your strategies in response to the feedback and insights you receive. To guarantee that you can effectively respond to shifting consumer demands and market circumstances, maintain an agile and flexible strategy.

You may put yourself in a position for long-term success and sustainable growth by handling the difficulties that come with growing your company. Accept the opportunities that come with expansion, and keep pushing the boundaries of innovation and development. Your entrepreneurial goals can be accomplished and the scaling process navigated with confidence if you have a growth mentality and a strong foundation.

NAVIGATING LEGAL AND REGULATORY REQUIREMENTS

10.1 Comprehending Legal Structures in Business

It is essential to comprehend the many legal structures that are available to you when launching a business. Selecting the appropriate legal framework for your company is crucial since it will define your liability, your tax duties, and the governance of your company. We will examine the various business legal structures in this area to assist you in making an informed choice that fits your needs and objectives.

10.1.1 Ownership by Oneself

The most basic type of business ownership is a sole proprietorship. Under this arrangement, a single person owns and runs the company. You have total authority over your company's operations as a lone owner. Your personal assets are in danger in the event that the business experiences financial difficulties because you are personally responsible for all of the company's debts and commitments.

The simplicity and affordability of starting a sole proprietorship are two benefits. You don't have to register your company with the government, but depending on your industry, you might need to get any required licenses or permissions. Furthermore, your personal income tax return includes a report of all company gains and losses.

It's crucial to remember, though, that a sole

proprietorship might not be the best option for companies that want to raise outside capital or have a significant liability risk. A solo proprietorship might also be difficult to grow because of how much of the owner's resources and abilities are needed.

10.1.2 Collaboration

A partnership is a type of legal arrangement in which two or more people jointly own and run a firm. General partnerships and limited partnerships are the two primary categories of partnerships.

Each member of a general partnership bears equal accountability and liability for the company. In addition to sharing in the company's gains and losses, each partner is also individually responsible for the partnership's debts and liabilities. A partnership agreement outlining the obligations, roles, and profit-sharing schedules of the partners must be in place.

A limited partnership, on the other hand, is made up of limited and general partners. Limited partners have limited liability and are usually passive investors, whereas general partners have unlimited liability and participate actively in the business's operations. Limited partners' responsibility is capped at the amount they have invested, and they are not involved in the day-to-day operations of the company.

The benefit of pooled resources, abilities, and knowledge is provided via partnerships. They also make joint decision-making and a more adaptable management structure possible. To prevent future disagreements and conflicts, it's crucial to pick your partners carefully and have a well-defined partnership agreement in place.

10.1.3 Business

A corporation and its shareholders are two different legal entities. Articles of incorporation are filed with the relevant government body to establish it. The owners of corporations, in contrast to sole proprietorships and partnerships, have limited liability, which shields their private assets from the liabilities and debts of the company.

Companies are managed by a board of directors that is chosen by the shareholders and has a more intricate structure. The officials in charge of the day-to-day operations of the company are chosen by the board of directors. Shareholders receive shares of stock from corporations, which are tradable and indicate ownership in the business.

The ability of a corporation to raise money through the sale of stock is one of its primary advantages. Furthermore, corporations are eternal entities, meaning that ownership changes won't affect their ability to function. On the other hand, businesses have additional rules and requirements, like having frequent shareholder meetings and keeping thorough financial records.

10.1.4 Company with Limited Liability (LLC)
Entities that combine the advantages of corporations and partnerships are called limited liability companies (LLCs). It offers its owners, referred to as members, limited liability protection along with management and taxation freedom. An operating agreement that specifies each member's obligations and rights governs LLCs.

Members of an LLC may elect to be taxed as corporations, partnerships, or sole proprietorships. Members can choose the most beneficial tax treatment for their business thanks to this flexibility. Moreover, compared to corporations, LLCs are subject to fewer formalities and reporting obligations.

Limited liability protection is one of the main benefits that an LLC provides to its members. This indicates that members' private assets are typically shielded from the liabilities and debts of the corporation. Additionally, LLCs offer flexibility with regard to management structure and profit distribution.

In summary
Selecting the appropriate legal framework for your company is a crucial choice that will affect its operations, liabilities, and taxation. Before choosing a legal structure, it is crucial to carefully assess your unique demands and speak with

financial and legal experts. Each legal structure has pros and cons of its own. Understanding the various business legal structures can help you make sure your company is compliant with all applicable rules and regulations and is positioned for success.

10.2 Registering Your Company and Getting Permits

Knowing the legal and regulatory requirements of beginning and running a business is essential once you have created a strong business plan and are prepared to implement your idea. To make sure your enterprise is legal and can run effectively, registering your firm and acquiring the required permits is a crucial first step. In this section, we will go over how to register your company and get the licenses necessary for your particular industry.

10.2.1 Selecting a Company Organization

Selecting the best legal structure for your enterprise is a prerequisite to registering your business. The kind of business structure you create will affect your company's overall management, liability, and taxation. The limited liability company (LLC), corporation, partnership, and sole proprietorship are the most popular forms of business organization. Every structure has benefits and drawbacks of its own, so in order to make an informed choice, thoroughly analyze your unique circumstances and speak with an accountant or lawyer.

10.2.2 Registering Your Company

The next step is to register your firm with the right government agencies after you have decided on the best business structure. Depending on where you live, the registration procedure may differ, but in general, you will need to fill out the proper documents and pay the required costs. Usually, this entails giving information about your company, like its name, address, ownership information, and the kind of business activities it engages in. It is crucial to confirm that the name you have picked for your company is original and does not violate any already-existing copyrights or trademarks.

You can register your business in a lot of countries, either in person at the local business registration office or online via government portals. To guarantee a seamless registration process, it is advisable to verify the particular requirements and processes of your jurisdiction. Remember that certain businesses can have extra licensing requirements; we'll talk about such in the next section.

10.2.3 Getting Licenses and Permits Particular to

Your Industry

To operate lawfully, you might need to get licenses and permissions unique to your industry, depending on the type of firm. These licenses, which are normally granted by governmental organizations or regulatory authorities, are intended to guarantee that companies abide by rules and guidelines particular to their industry. The exact licenses and permits needed will change based on where you live and the kind of business you run.

For instance, you would probably need to get liquor licenses, food handling permits, and health permits if you were opening a restaurant. You might need to get licenses in relation to building codes and safety requirements if you're starting a construction company. It is essential to learn about and comprehend the licensing requirements particular to your business in order to stay out of trouble with the law and avoid penalties.

You will normally need to file an application, present supporting documentation, and pay the needed costs in order to receive the required licenses and permits. Depending on your business, the application procedure may include background checks, inspections, and interviews. In order to guarantee that you have all the required licenses and permits in place before you start operations, it is crucial to start this procedure well in advance.

10.2.4 Protection of Intellectual Property

It's critical to think about intellectual property protection in addition to business registration and license acquisition. The term "intellectual property" describes mental products including inventions, designs, trade names, and creative works. Your ideas can't be used or profited from by others without your permission if you safeguard your intellectual property.

There are various ways to safeguard intellectual property, such as trade secrets, copyrights, trademarks, and patents. New technologies and ideas are protected by patents; brand names and logos are protected by trademarks; original creative works are protected by copyrights; and private company information is shielded by trade secrets. You might need to think about applying for one or more of these protections, depending on the type of business you operate.

You may learn more about the most effective methods for safeguarding your intellectual property by speaking with an intellectual property lawyer. In the event that someone violates your intellectual property, they can assist you in enforcing your rights and guiding you through the application process.

10.2.5 Adherence to Labor and Tax Laws

Adherence to tax and employment rules is crucial for business owners in order to avoid legal complications and penalties. This entails knowing your tax responsibilities and registering for the necessary tax identification numbers, such as an Employer Identification Number (EIN) in the US. To make sure you are fulfilling all of your tax requirements and utilizing any applicable credits or deductions, it is advisable to speak with a tax expert or accountant.

In addition, you will have to abide by employment rules and regulations if you intend to hire staff. This entails confirming that your workers are legally permitted to work in your nation, paying the minimum wage, maintaining a secure workplace, and abiding by labor regulations. To ensure compliance, familiarize yourself with the employment regulations in your jurisdiction and think about obtaining legal counsel.

You are laying a solid foundation for your firm by registering it, getting the required licenses and permissions, safeguarding your intellectual property, and abiding by employment and tax rules. Although these legal and regulatory standards may seem overwhelming, your company's long-term success and survival depend on them. To make sure that your company runs lawfully and morally, take the time to comprehend these responsibilities, carry them out, and, if necessary, seek professional assistance.

10.3 Intellectual Property Protection

Any firm can greatly benefit from intellectual property (IP), which is the collection of intangible works of human creativity that includes innovations, designs, trademarks, and artistic works. Maintaining your competitive edge and making sure your company succeeds in the long run depend on protecting your intellectual property. This section will discuss the different types of intellectual property, how important it is to protect it, and some tactics you may use to keep your works and ideas protected.

10.3.1 Comprehending Intellectual Property

There are four primary categories of intellectual property: trade secrets, copyrights, trademarks, and patents. Every variety has a distinct function and offers varying degrees of security. Determining the right course of action to protect your intellectual property requires an understanding of these categories.

Patents: An innovation that is innovative and valuable might be granted exclusive rights to the inventor via a patent, which is a legal document. It gives the inventor the exclusive right to produce, use, and market the invention for a finite amount of time, usually 20 years. Businesses that depend on novel technologies or exclusive processes must have patents. They keep others from using your idea for their own gain without your consent.

Brands
Trademarks are identifying markers, such as names, logos, or symbols, that set one company's products or services apart from another. They act as a source of identification, promote brand awareness, and foster client loyalty. A trademark can be legally protected from unlawful use or infringement by third parties by registering it. Selecting a distinctive and unforgettable trademark is crucial to guaranteeing its efficacy in setting your company apart from competitors.

Copyright protection
Original works of authorship, such as plays, songs, artwork, and books, are safeguarded by copyright laws. It gives the author the only authority to make copies, give them away, exhibit them, and perform them. Although copyright protection is automatically granted at the time the work is created, registering your copyright has additional advantages, including the capacity to file a lawsuit for infringement and pursue statutory damages.

For companies that create creative stuff, such as software, books, music, or artwork, copyrights are essential.

Trade Secrets
Trade secrets are valuable and sensitive commercial information that provides a business with a competitive edge. Formulas, procedures, client lists, and marketing plans are a few examples of this. Trade secrets aren't made public like patents, trademarks, and copyrights are. Rather, they are shielded by internal security protocols and confidentiality agreements. Preserving trade secrets is crucial in order to stop rivals from obtaining important confidential data.

10.3.2 The Value of Intellectual Property Protection
For a number of reasons, it is essential to protect your intellectual property. In the first place, it keeps others from making money off of your labor of love by guaranteeing that you have exclusive rights to your discoveries, products, or brand identification. Second, it creates a competitive edge by setting your goods and services apart from those of your rivals. Thirdly, it raises the worth of your company because intellectual property can be a valuable asset when looking for collaborations or investments. Lastly, by preserving the integrity and reputation of your brand, you can make sure that consumers will continue to link your goods and services with excellence and innovation.

10.3.3 Methods of Intellectual Property Protection

You must use a mix of internal procedures, proactive tactics, and legal measures to safeguard your intellectual property. Here are some crucial tactics to think about:

Perform an entire intellectual property assessment.

To discover and evaluate all the intellectual property assets your company has, start with an IP audit. Trade secrets, copyrights, patents, and trademarks are all included in this. Assess the worth and any dangers connected to every asset. With the aid of this audit, you may create a thorough plan and prioritize your IP protection actions.

Submit an Application for Protection of Intellectual Property.

To obtain exclusive rights for inventions or special procedures, think about submitting a patent application. To make sure your innovation satisfies the requirements and to successfully navigate the challenging patent application procedure, collaborate with a patent attorney. To safeguard your brand identification and stop others from utilizing marks that are similar to yours, register your trademarks. Your creative works should be protected by a copyright to ensure legal ownership and prevent unlawful usage. Seek advice from attorneys who focus on intellectual property law to make sure you adhere to all rules and regulations.

Put in place non-disclosure and confidentiality agreements.
Use confidentiality and non-disclosure agreements (NDAs) with workers, contractors, and business partners to safeguard trade secrets and private information. The parties to these agreements are legally obligated to protect sensitive information's confidentiality and guard against its unlawful use or disclosure. Clearly state what information is considered secret and what happens if the agreement is broken.

Keep an eye on and defend your rights.
Keep an eye out for any possible violations of your intellectual property rights in the market on a regular basis. This entails keeping an eye on trade exhibits, industry magazines, and internet platforms. In the event that you find any violations, act quickly to protect your rights. This could entail suing people, submitting cease-and-desist letters, or using alternate conflict resolution procedures. Collaborate closely with attorneys who specialize in intellectual property law to guarantee that your rights are adequately safeguarded and upheld.

Teach and develop your staff.
Inform your staff and associates of the value of protecting intellectual property and their part in ensuring its protection. Give instructions on how to recognize and handle private information,

spot possible violations, and report any issues. A culture of intellectual property awareness can help reduce the likelihood of inadvertent disclosures or improper use of private data.

Keep records and documentation up-to-date.
Maintain thorough records of all of your intellectual property assets, such as copyright paperwork, patent applications, trademark registrations, and registration certificates. Keep all pertinent documents in one convenient location, and make sure they are easily accessible. As your intellectual property portfolio changes, make sure to periodically check and update these records.

In summary
Keeping your intellectual property safe is essential to growing your company. You can protect your concepts, innovations, and brand identification by comprehending the many forms of intellectual property and putting the right plans into action. In order to make sure you follow the right procedures and fulfill all legal obligations, don't forget to speak with legal experts who specialize in intellectual property. You may safeguard your competitive advantage, raise the value of your company, and lay a solid foundation for long-term success by safeguarding your intellectual property.

10.4 Adhering to Labor and Tax Laws

Understanding and abiding by tax and employment rules is essential for entrepreneurs in order to maintain the smooth operation of their businesses. Violations of these regulations may incur harsh fines and legal repercussions. This section will examine the important facets of employment and tax laws that you should be aware of and offer advice on how to effectively manage them.

10.4.1 Recognizing Your Tax Liabilities

Keeping up with tax requirements is one of a business owner's main duties. This entails being aware of the many tax categories that apply to your company and making sure that your paperwork is filed on time and accurately. The following are some important taxes to be mindful of:

Tax on income
An income tax is a tax that is applied to the money

that your business makes. The legal structure of your company may affect the tax rate and laws. Maintaining comprehensive documentation of your business's earnings and outlays is crucial for precisely computing your taxable income.

VAT on sales

A tax levied on the sale of goods and services is known as a sales tax. Each jurisdiction has its own sales tax rates and laws. It is critical to ascertain whether your company must collect and pay sales tax, as well as to comprehend the associated reporting and filing obligations.

Payroll Taxes

Payroll taxes must be withheld and remitted on behalf of any employees you may have. Payroll taxes comprise Social Security and Medicare taxes, as well as withholding from federal and state income taxes. Precisely computing and deducting the right amount from your workers' pay and sending it to the relevant tax authorities is crucial.

Employer-Self Tax

In the event that you are an individual or a partner in a partnership, you might have to pay self-employment tax. This tax is computed using your net self-employment income and is comparable to Social Security and Medicare taxes. Comprehending your self-employment tax responsibilities and fulfilling your payment deadlines are crucial.

10.4.2 Hiring Workers and Labor Laws

It is essential to get knowledgeable about employment regulations before making any hiring decisions in order to maintain compliance and establish a fair and productive workplace. Here are some important things to think about:

Contracts of employment

Written employment contracts that specify the terms and conditions of work are advised. Important topics such as job duties, pay, perks, working hours, and termination procedures should all be covered in these contracts. Speak with an employment lawyer to make sure your contracts adhere to regional labor laws.

Overtime and Minimum Wage Regulations

Make sure you are paying your workers the minimum wage required by any applicable local, state, or federal legislation. Study up on overtime rules as well. These mandate that firms compensate qualified workers for overtime when their hours exceed a predetermined level. It is imperative to adhere to these laws in order to prevent legal conflicts and fines.

laws against discrimination

The laws against discrimination in the workplace are very strong. Learn about the anti-discrimination laws that shield workers from being treated unfairly on the basis of their color, gender, age, religion, handicap, or country of origin. Adopt procedures and policies that support fairness and guard against discrimination in the workplace.

Benefits and Leave Policies for Employees
You can be obliged to offer specific perks to your employees, such as paid time off, retirement programs, and health insurance, depending on the size and type of your company. Make sure you are giving your staff the perks they are entitled to and familiarizing yourself with the relevant rules and regulations.

10.4.3 Reporting and Documentation
Compliance with employment and tax laws depends on keeping accurate and well-organized records. Observe the following recommended practices:

All financial transactions, including income, expenses, and payroll, should be meticulously documented.
All tax filings, including payroll tax returns, sales tax returns, and income tax returns, should be kept on file.
Keep track of all employee documentation, such as payroll records, time and attendance logs, and employment contracts.
To guarantee accuracy and compliance with evolving rules and regulations, check and update your records on a regular basis.
10.4.4 Seeking Expert Advice
It can be difficult to navigate employment and tax rules, particularly if you are not familiar with

the requirements. Consultation with accountants, tax consultants, and employment attorneys is strongly advised. These specialists can guide you through the complexities of complying with employment and tax laws and offer professional advice tailored to your unique business requirements.

You can shield your company from legal problems and foster a healthy work environment for your employees by being aware of and abiding by employment and tax rules. Spend some time familiarizing yourself with these laws, and when necessary, seek professional advice. Adherence to tax and employment regulations is a crucial component of fostering your enterprise and guaranteeing its sustained prosperity.

MANAGING RISKS AND OVERCOMING CHALLENGES

11.1 Recognizing and Evaluating Business Hazards

It is essential for entrepreneurs to realize that there are dangers associated with every business endeavor. A crucial first step in growing your organization is recognizing and evaluating these risks. You may improve your chances of success and lessen the effect of possible obstacles by being proactive and organized.

11.1.1 Comprehending Business Hazards

Risks associated with your business can come from a variety of sources and can seriously affect your endeavor. To effectively manage these risks, a thorough understanding of them is necessary. These are a few typical categories of business risks:

Market risk is the kind of risk that results from modifications to the market environment, such as changes in customer preferences, recessions, or the entry of new rivals. You may reduce market risks by being aware of industry developments and having a thorough understanding of your target market.

Financial Risk: A few examples of financial risks are cash flow issues, funding difficulties, and unforeseen costs. To reduce these risks, it is essential to have a sound financial strategy in place and to often check your financial performance.

Operational Risk: These risks are related to the regular business activities that you conduct. These hazards may include staff mistakes, supply chain interruptions, or equipment failure. Reducing operational risks can be achieved by putting in place efficient operating procedures and having backup plans.

Legal and Regulatory Risk: Any organization must adhere to all applicable laws and regulations. Fines, legal issues, or reputational harm may arise from breaking laws and regulations. Legal and regulatory risks can be reduced by being aware of the legal and regulatory environment that applies to your business and by consulting a specialist.

Technology Risk: Given the current digital era, there is a growing prevalence of technology dangers. Data breaches, antiquated IT infrastructure, and cybersecurity threats are a few examples of these dangers. Technology hazards can be reduced by putting strong cybersecurity measures in place and keeping up with new developments.

11.1.2 Evaluating Business Hazards
Assessing the possibility and potential impact of the risks that your firm may encounter comes next after you have identified them. You may better manage these risks by allocating resources and setting priorities with the aid of this assessment. To evaluate business risks, follow these steps:

Risk Identification: To begin, compile a thorough inventory of all the possible hazards that your company might encounter. Take into account all potential external and internal influences on your project.

Risk Probability: Evaluate the possibility that each risk will materialize. To estimate the likelihood of each risk, take into account past performance, current market trends, and professional judgment.

Risk Impact: Consider the possible effects of any risk on your company. Take into account elements like monetary loss, harm to one's reputation, or interruptions to operations. Based on the possible consequences of each risk, rate its severity.

Risk Prioritization: Sort the hazards according to likelihood and significance. Pay close attention to the dangers that could seriously affect your company and have a high likelihood of happening.

Strategies for Mitigating Risks: Formulate plans to alleviate each danger that has been identified. These tactics could be putting preventive measures into place, making backup plans, or shifting the risk through partnerships or insurance.

Monitoring and Review: Keep a close eye on your risk mitigation techniques' efficacy. As new hazards materialize or as current risks change, update your risk assessment.

You can take proactive steps to lessen business risks' negative effects on your endeavor by methodically identifying and evaluating them. Keep in mind that risk assessment is a continuous process, and as your company grows, it is critical to periodically review and update your risk management plans.

11.1.3 Overcoming Typical Obstacles in Entrepreneurship

Throughout their journey, entrepreneurs frequently encounter a variety of obstacles in addition to risk management. Your tenacity and resolve may be put to the test by these difficulties. The following are some typical obstacles faced by entrepreneurs and how to overcome them:

Uncertainty: There is a lot of uncertainty when starting a business. Accept uncertainty as a chance for development and education. Remain flexible and prepared to change course as needed.

Limited Resources: Having insufficient funds, labor, or time can be very difficult. Set priorities for your resources and concentrate on the tasks that will affect your company most significantly. To make the most of your resources, look for innovative ideas and make use of alliances.

Competition: In any industry, competition is unavoidable. Offer distinctive value propositions, first-rate customer support, or cutting-edge goods and services to set your company apart. Keep a close eye on your rivals and stay abreast of market developments.

Managing Growth: Growing your company can present both opportunities and difficulties. Make sure your staff, procedures, and infrastructure can manage the extra workload. Seek advice from seasoned mentors or advisors who have made it through comparable growth stages.

Work-Life Balance: Being an entrepreneur may be hard, and it frequently makes it difficult to distinguish between work and personal time. Establish limits and prioritize self-care in order to preserve a positive work-life balance. Assemble a team that is encouraging and provides responsibilities to others.

Keep in mind that obstacles are a necessary component of the entrepreneurial path. Accept them as chances for development and education. Through cultivating resilience, obtaining assistance, and maintaining goal focus, you can surmount these obstacles and attain achievement.

11.1.4 Adjusting to Shifts and Upheavals in the Market

Market shifts and disruptions are unavoidable, and the business environment is always changing. To secure the long-term viability of your business, it is imperative that you, as an entrepreneur, remain flexible and adjust to these developments. The following tactics can assist you in navigating shifts and disruptions in the market:

Remain Up to Date: Keep abreast of developments in technology, market trends, and customer behavior. Do market research on a regular basis to find new prospects and possible dangers.

Embrace Innovation: Encourage an innovative culture in your company. Motivate your group to experiment and think beyond the box. To stay ahead of the curve, embrace innovative technologies and modify your business approach.

Customer-Centric Approach: Pay close attention to your consumers' changing demands and preferences. To satisfy their shifting needs, modify your offerings in terms of goods, services, and marketing plans.

Form Strategic Alliances: Work together with other companies or industry leaders to take advantage of their knowledge, connections, and resources. You can more skillfully handle market shifts and disruptions with the aid of strategic alliances.

Always Learn: Make an investment in your own advancement, both personally and professionally. Seek advice from mentors or advisors, participate in conferences and workshops, and stay current on industry best practices. You'll gain the information and abilities necessary to adjust to changes in the industry through ongoing learning.

Through adapting to change, remaining knowledgeable, and consistently pursuing innovation, you may set up your company for success in a dynamic and constantly shifting market.

In summary, one of the most important aspects of growing your company is recognizing and evaluating business risks. You may lessen the impact of possible difficulties by being aware of the many kinds of risks, evaluating their likelihood and impact, and creating efficient risk mitigation plans. You can also set up your company for long-term success by conquering typical entrepreneurial obstacles, adjusting to market shifts and upheavals, and maintaining flexibility. Keep in mind that becoming an entrepreneur is a journey with ups and downs. You may grow as an entrepreneur and accomplish your business goals by accepting the challenges and learning from them.

11.2 Formulating Techniques for Risk Mitigation

It is crucial for entrepreneurs to realize that there are dangers involved in launching and operating a firm. These risks can take many different forms, including difficulties with finances, operations, the law, or the market. Although it is not feasible to completely remove hazards, you may lessen their effects and raise the likelihood that your firm will succeed by using effective risk mitigation techniques.

11.2.1 Recognizing Possible Dangers

The identification of potential hazards that your company may encounter is the first step in creating risk mitigation measures. This entails carrying out an exhaustive examination of your company's operations, market patterns, and outside variables that might have an effect on your enterprise. Among the typical dangers that business owners frequently face are:

Risks to Money

Risks associated with finances include problems with funding, cash flow, and profitability. These risks may include insufficient funding, unforeseen costs, or downturns in the economy that jeopardize the stability of your company's finances.

Risks Associated with Operations

Operational hazards are related to the daily activities that your company conducts. These risks may affect the productivity and efficiency of your organization and include problems with manufacturing, supply chain disruptions, technological malfunctions, or personnel blunders.

Risks to Law and Compliance

Risks related to legality and compliance include the possibility that your company will run afoul of the law or fail to follow applicable rules and regulations. Lawsuits, intellectual property violations, and breaking employment or tax regulations are a few examples of these dangers.

Risks in the Market

Market risks include things like shifting consumer tastes, rivalry, and general economic conditions that could have an impact on your company's capacity to draw in new clients and keep existing ones. These risks may include modifications to industry legislation, new competitors entering the market, or changes in consumer behavior.

11.2.2 Determining and Sorting Out the Risks

The next stage after identifying potential hazards is to evaluate and rank them according to how likely they are to occur and how they might affect your company. This entails calculating the likelihood that each risk will materialize as well as the possible effects it might have on the day-to-day operations, financial situation, public perception, and overall performance of your company.

To properly evaluate risks, take into account the following elements:

Probability

Calculate the likelihood that each risk will materialize using past experience, industry trends, and professional judgment. Give each risk a score, such as low, medium, or high, to reflect the possibility that it may materialize.

Effect

Consider each risk's possible effects on your company. Think about the possible effects on finances, operations, the law, and reputation. Give each risk a score, such as low, medium, or high, to reflect the seriousness of the potential consequences.

Priority of Risk

Prioritize risks by combining the likelihood and impact ratings. High-priority risks should be addressed first because they represent the biggest danger to the success of your company. Create mitigation plans for every risk that has been identified, giving top emphasis to the most important ones first.

11.2.3 Formulating Techniques for Risk Mitigation

It's time to create efficient risk mitigation techniques after you have determined which hazards are most important and ranked them. These tactics are designed to lessen the chance of hazards materializing or to lessen their effects in the event that they do. When creating risk-reduction plans, keep the following important steps in mind:

1. Avoiding risks

Risks that have a high probability and a serious consequence should be completely avoided. This could entail making calculated choices like passing up on certain business prospects or going after markets that carry a high risk for your company.

2. Transfer of Risk

Certain risks may be assigned to third parties by means of contracts or insurance coverage. For instance, you can give an insurance company control over the risk of liability or property damage. Examine and negotiate contracts carefully to make sure that the parties have agreed upon a fair distribution of risks.

3. Mitigation of Risk

Put policies in place to lessen the chance or

effect of hazards that have been recognized. This could entail putting in place redundancies, backup systems, or safety procedures to lessen the effects of technological or operational breakdowns. To reduce the possibility of staff errors, conduct frequent training sessions and performance reviews.

4. Planning for Risk Contingencies
Create backup plans in case there are risks that cannot be totally mitigated or avoided. These plans specify what should be done in case of a risk occurrence so that your company can react appropriately and reduce the impact on daily operations.

5. Consistent observation and evaluation
Strategies for mitigating risk shouldn't be rigidly prescribed. Make necessary modifications to your strategies based on a regular evaluation and monitoring of their efficacy. Keep abreast of market developments, legislative adjustments, and new risks to make sure your risk mitigation tactics are current and efficient.

11.2.4 Explaining and Putting Risk Mitigation Plans into Practice
It is imperative to effectively communicate and implement your developed risk mitigation strategies throughout your organization. This includes:

1. Awareness and Training of Employees

Make certain that every worker is informed about the hazards that have been identified and the appropriate mitigation techniques. Employees can better understand their roles and responsibilities in risk mitigation by receiving training and resources.

2. Unambiguous Lines of Communication
Create open lines of communication within your company to make it easier for people to report possible risks and put mitigation plans into action. Urge staff members to promptly report any risks or issues.

3. Frequent Assessment and Documentation
Make sure you regularly assess the success of your risk-reduction tactics and report back to relevant parties. This promotes confidence in your company's capacity to successfully manage risks.

4. Ongoing Enhancement
Always look for ways to make your risk-reduction tactics better. As your company grows and new risks present themselves, take lessons from the past and modify your plans accordingly.

You can anticipate problems and strengthen your company's resilience by creating and putting into practice efficient risk mitigation plans. To ensure long-term success, keep in mind that risk management is a continuous process that needs to be incorporated into your entire business plan.

11.3 Overcoming Typical Obstacles in Entrepreneurship

Establishing and maintaining a firm has its share of difficulties. Being an entrepreneur means that you will unavoidably encounter challenges that will put your perseverance and fortitude to the test. You may, however, overcome these obstacles and keep moving forward on your successful journey if you have the appropriate attitude and techniques. This section will examine several typical entrepreneurial obstacles and offer helpful suggestions for resolving them.

11.3.1 Cash Flow Management

Managing cash flow is one of the most frequent problems that entrepreneurs encounter. Any firm depends on cash flow, and even successful ones can experience financial troubles if they are not managed well. Creating a sound financial strategy and budget is essential to overcoming this obstacle. This entails projecting your income and expenses with accuracy, keeping a close eye on your financial flow, and making necessary modifications. To maintain a healthy cash flow, you can also think about putting tactics into place like negotiating advantageous payment terms with suppliers, rewarding early payments from clients, and looking into alternate financing possibilities.

11.3.2 Developing a Robust Clientele

Any business's long-term success depends on gaining and keeping clients. But drawing clients can be very difficult, particularly in a cutthroat industry. The key to overcoming this obstacle is creating a thorough marketing plan that precisely targets your ideal clients. This entails determining who your target audience is, learning about their wants and requirements, and developing persuasive marketing messages that appeal to them. To reach your target demographic and develop a solid client base, make use of a variety of marketing platforms, including social media, content marketing, and search engine optimization.

11.3.3 Getting Used to New Technology

In the modern, technologically advanced world, businesses rely heavily on technology to succeed. But staying current with technology may be difficult, particularly for small companies with little funding. It's critical to keep up with the most recent technical advancements and trends in your sector if you want to overcome this obstacle. Examine your company's procedures on a regular basis to find places where technology might increase productivity and streamline processes. Accept new technologies that complement your company objectives and make training and development investments to guarantee that your staff is equipped to take advantage of these developments.

11.3.4 Handling Expansion

Although most entrepreneurs see expansion as their ultimate aim, managing quick development can come with its own set of difficulties. Careful planning and execution are necessary when scaling a firm to make sure that the resources and infrastructure are able to handle the additional demand. It is crucial to plan ahead for future expansion obstacles and create a scalability strategy early on in order to overcome this difficulty. This could entail making strategic alliances, investing in infrastructure and technology, and recruiting more employees. To successfully manage and sustain growth, review key performance indicators on a regular basis and make necessary adjustments to your strategies.

11.3.5 Handling Risk and Uncertainty

Since entrepreneurship is, by its very nature, dangerous, entrepreneurs must constantly find ways to manage uncertainty. Identifying possible risks and outlining mitigation strategies are crucial components of a risk management strategy that will help you overcome this obstacle. This includes carrying out a comprehensive risk assessment, putting risk mitigation strategies into place, and routinely evaluating and revising your risk management plan. Furthermore, developing a resilient and adaptive attitude will support you in navigating unpredictable times and making wise choices when faced with danger.

11.3.6 Juggling Personal and Professional Life
Your personal life may suffer as a result of the hard work and devotion that come with becoming an entrepreneur. For entrepreneurs, juggling work and personal obligations is a frequent struggle. It is critical to establish limits and give self-care first priority in order to overcome this obstacle. Assign duties and obligations to your group, create a timetable that accommodates personal time, and set aside time for self-renewing activities. Recall that long-term success and general well-being depend on you maintaining a healthy work-life balance.

11.3.7 Creating a Robust Group
Creating a solid and resilient workforce is essential to any company's success. However, it can be difficult to attract and retain excellent people, particularly for small and beginning companies. To overcome this difficulty, it is crucial to invest in your team's development and build a healthy and inclusive work culture. Offer competitive wages

and benefits, create possibilities for growth and progress, and cultivate open communication and collaboration. By providing an environment where employees feel valued and supported, you can recruit and keep top talent who will contribute to the success of your organization.

11.3.8 Seeking Support and Mentorship

Entrepreneurship can sometimes feel like a lonely road, but finding help and guidance can make a major impact. Surround yourself with a network of like-minded entrepreneurs who can provide advice, support, and useful insights. Join industry associations, attend networking events, and seek out mentorship possibilities. Learning from the experiences of others who have faced similar issues can help you handle obstacles more efficiently and accelerate your business growth.

In conclusion, entrepreneurship is a rewarding yet tough journey. By recognizing and proactively tackling typical entrepreneurial difficulties, you can boost your chances of success. Develop ways to manage cash flow, build a solid customer base, adapt to technological advancements, manage growth, cope with uncertainty and risk, balance work and personal life, build a resilient team, and seek help and mentorship. With tenacity, determination, and a desire to learn and adapt, you may overcome these hurdles and achieve your entrepreneurial ambitions.

11.4 Adjusting to Shifts and Upheavals in the Market

In the dynamic world of business, change is unavoidable. Disruptive innovations arise, markets evolve, and consumer preferences shift. To be competitive and guarantee the long-term success of your company, it is imperative that you, as an entrepreneur, not only foresee these changes but also make the necessary adjustments to accommodate them. We will look at tactics and best practices in this section for responding to shifts and disruptions in the market.

11.4.1 Adopting a Growth Perspective

A growth mentality is necessary to adjust to market disruptions and changes. This kind of thinking is defined by an openness to new ideas, a readiness to learn, and a constant pursuit of improvement. You can view market shifts as opportunities for growth rather than as roadblocks if you adopt a growth mentality. Adopt a curious attitude and be willing to consider new options. Keep up with developments in emerging technology, consumer behavior, and industry trends. This will let you see possible hiccups and modify your operations accordingly.

11.4.2 Keeping an Eye on the Market

You need to be up-to-date on the newest trends and advancements in your business in order to adjust to changes in the market. Keep a close eye on consumer preferences, rivalry, and market conditions. Market research, industry conferences, industry expert networking, and internet resource utilization can all help achieve this. You may proactively detect changes in the market and modify your business tactics by staying ahead of the curve.

11.4.3 Including Flexibility in Your Company's Strategy

Including flexibility in your business plan is essential for responding to market shifts. It may be challenging to adjust traditional company models to changing market conditions since they are inflexible and resistant to change. Think about embracing ideas like design thinking or the lean startup technique to take a more agile approach. These frameworks put a strong emphasis on client input, experimentation, and iteration, which enables you to quickly pivot and adjust your business in reaction to changes in the market.

11.4.4 Taking Innovation Head-On

Innovation is an effective strategy for responding to disruptions and changes in the market. You may promote innovative thinking and problem-solving within your company by cultivating an innovative culture. Motivate your group to question the status quo, investigate novel concepts, and think creatively. Accept new trends and technology that have the power to upend your sector. You can keep ahead of the competition and adjust to changes in the market more skillfully if you are always coming up with new ideas.

11.4.5 Establishing Powerful Alliances

In a market that is evolving quickly, it might be difficult for one company to stay on top of everything. Creating strategic alliances will make it easier for you to deal with disruptions and changes in the market. Seek out chances to work together with other companies, industry professionals, or even rival companies. By combining your resources, skills, and knowledge, you can take advantage of group advantages to adjust to shifting market conditions and grab fresh chances.

11.4.6 Stressing Input from Customers

You can learn a lot from your customers about how to adjust your business and comprehend changes in the industry. Engage in active customer feedback gathering via focus groups, surveys, and social media monitoring. Be mindful of their evolving requirements, inclinations, and areas of discomfort. Make informed judgments about product development, marketing tactics, and general business matters by utilizing this input. You can modify your business to match your clients' changing expectations if you maintain a close relationship with them.

11.4.7 Ongoing Education and Talent Advancement

To keep up with the ever-changing economy, one must always be learning and developing new skills. By reading, going to workshops, or enrolling in online courses, you may stay current on business trends, emerging technology, and industry best practices. Encourage the members of your team to participate in professional development initiatives. Gaining more knowledge and expertise will help you better navigate changing market conditions and position your company for success.

11.4.8 Quickness and Agility in Making Decisions

A market that is evolving quickly demands flexibility and swift decision-making. Create a structure for decision-making that enables you to act swiftly and decisively. This may include giving trusted team members the power to make decisions, establishing explicit standards for decision-making, or using analytics and data to guide your choices. You can react to changes in the market and take advantage of new chances more quickly if you are quick to make decisions and flexible.

11.4.9 Leaning into Digital

Technology may greatly facilitate the process of responding to market fluctuations and disruptions. To increase customer satisfaction, streamline processes, and maintain an advantage over competitors, embrace digital transformation and make use of technology. Investigate cutting-edge technologies that could upend your sector, such as blockchain, artificial intelligence, and the Internet of Things. By utilizing technology, you can modify your company to satisfy your clients' shifting wants and maintain your position as a market leader.

11.4.10 Fostering an Adaptive Culture

Finally, fostering a culture of flexibility is essential to effectively managing shifts and disruptions in the market. Motivate your group to accept change, take measured chances, and grow from mistakes. Encourage the creation of an atmosphere that values creativity and exploration. Establishing a culture that encourages flexibility will enable your staff to take proactive measures in response to changes in the market and propel your company's growth.

It takes constant attention to detail, flexibility, and an openness to adapt to market upheavals and changes. You may position your company for long-term success in a market that is always changing by embracing innovation, using a growth mentality, remaining informed, and incorporating flexibility into your business plan. Recall that in the fast-paced corporate world of today, the capacity for adaptation is not only a necessary survival skill but also a competitive advantage.

LAUNCHING YOUR BUSINESS

12.1 Crafting an Iconic Launch Plan

An exciting and significant step in your

entrepreneurial career is launching your business. It is the result of your extensive preparation, study, and labor of love. Your company may build a solid foundation and lay the groundwork for future growth with a successful launch. This section will cover the essential components of developing an engaging launch strategy that will enthrall your target market and build buzz about your company.

12.1.1 Specifying Your Launch Goals

It's crucial to establish your goals before getting into the finer points of your launch strategy. What do you want your launch to accomplish? Are you hoping to get attention from the media and create buzz, draw in new clients, or position your company as an industry leader? Setting clear objectives can assist you in developing your launch strategy and gauging its effectiveness.

12.1.2 Recognizing Your Target Audience

You must have a thorough understanding of your target market in order to design a memorable launch. Who do they represent? What are their wants, requirements, and areas of discomfort? To learn more about the preferences, habits, and demographics of your target audience, conduct in-depth market research. You may use this information to help you create a launch strategy that appeals to and engages your target audience.

12.1.3 Developing a Brand Narrative

The tale that binds your audience to your company is known as your brand story. Your mission, values, and USP are all communicated through it. A strong brand narrative has the power to stir feelings and leave a lasting effect. Make the most of your launch to share your brand's narrative and build a strong emotional bond with your target audience. Write a story that highlights your experience, the issue you're trying to solve, and the change you want to see.

12.1.4 Constructing Expectations

Building anticipation is a great method to get people talking about your launch and becoming excited. By providing your audience with unique previews, behind-the-scenes videos, and sneak peeks, you can start generating anticipation far in advance. Use your website, email marketing, and social media accounts to generate interest and suspense. Think about holding giveaways, competitions, or one-time deals to encourage your audience to interact with your brand before it launches.

12.1.5 Making the Most of Partnerships and Influencers

Strategic alliances and influencers can greatly boost your launch efforts. Choose industry insiders or influencers with a sizable following who share the same values as your company. Work together to produce content, organize events, or provide product or service endorsements. Additionally, look for alliances with like-minded companies or groups that might aid in extending your reach and drawing in more customers.

12.1.6 Making Eye-Catching Content

A key component of your launch plan is content. Create a content strategy that consists of press releases, blog entries, videos, and social media content. Your writing needs to be interesting, educational, and shared. Employ narrative strategies to draw in customers and emphasize the distinctive features of your company. Think about producing a series of instructional materials or a countdown to the launch.

12.1.7 Organizing a Commendable Launch Party

A launch party can be an effective means of giving your audience an experience they won't soon forget. Make sure the event fits with your brand and appeals to your target audience, whether it's a virtual, live, or hybrid event. Create interesting events, invite thought leaders or influential people in the business to speak, and allow guests a chance to engage with your goods or services. Remember to take pictures and videos of the event to post on your website and social media accounts.

12.1.8 Interacting with the Press

The exposure of your brand and your launch efforts can both be greatly enhanced by media coverage. Create a press kit, write press releases, and contact relevant bloggers, influencers, and journalists as part of a media outreach campaign. Make your pitches unique and emphasize the parts of your company that your target audience would find interesting. Have your main points of emphasis and talking points ready for any media interviews.

12.1.9 Tracking and Assessing Achievement

After your launch has started, it is critical to track and evaluate its progress. Establish key performance indicators (KPIs) in line with the goals of your launch. Keep an eye on data like website traffic, social media interaction, media mentions, and client reviews. Examine the information and modify your plan of action if necessary. Honor your accomplishments and draw lessons from any obstacles or failures.

12.1.10 Constantly Adapting Your Launch Plan

A launch is merely the start of your entrepreneurial adventure. Make constant changes to your launch plan based on the insights and comments you receive from your target audience. Adjust to shifting consumer tastes, market trends, and industry developments. Remain adaptable and willing to try new things. A launch strategy has to be a dynamic document that changes as your company does.

You'll be well on your way to effectively exposing your business to the world if you adhere to these guidelines and make the effort to develop an unforgettable launch strategy. Recall that a well-managed launch can build a solid foundation for your company and pave the way for expansion in the future. I wish you luck!

12.2 Carrying Out a Fruitful Product Launch

After your product has been produced and you are prepared to launch it, it is time to carry out a successful product launch. An effective launch may build anticipation, generate buzz, and propel early sales for your company. We will examine the essential procedures and tactics in this section to guarantee a fruitful product launch.

12.2.1 Clearly Defining Launch Objectives

Prior to launching your product, it's critical to establish certain objectives. What do you want your launch to accomplish? Are you trying to reach a specific sales target, get attention from the media, or build brand awareness? You can coordinate your launch strategy and tactics by clearly identifying your objectives.

12.2.2 Constructing Expectations

One of the most important elements of a successful product launch is creating anticipation. It is important to create anticipation and a buzz about your product even before it is released onto the market. The following are some techniques to create anticipation:

Teaser Campaign: Develop a campaign that offers teasing information about your product but refrains from giving away too much. You can accomplish this by using countdowns on your website, email newsletters, and social media posts.

Influencer Collaborations: Join forces with professionals in the field or influencers who can help spread the word and excite a larger audience. They can provide content, tell others about their interactions with your product, and pique followers' interest.

Pre-Launch Events: Plan special previews or pre-launch events for a limited number of people. This can apply to the media, business insiders, or devoted patrons. You may create an air of exclusivity and early buzz by offering them a sneak peek.

12.2.3 Developing Captivating Messages
Create appealing messaging if you want to convey the benefits of your product and spark interest. Your marketing materials should succinctly state the issue your product resolves, as well as highlight its special qualities and advantages over competing products. Take into account these suggestions:

Specialized Selling Point (USP): Determine the USP of your product and emphasize it in your messaging. What distinguishes your product from rival offerings? Why should buyers pick your product above competing ones?

narrative: To captivate your audience and establish an emotional bond, use narrative strategies. Talk about the development process of your product, the issue it resolves, and the potential benefits to people's lives.

Clear and succinct: Make sure your message is easy to read, clear, and succinct. Steer clear of employing complicated or technical language that could turn off or confuse potential customers.

12.2.4 Making Use of Various Marketing Channels
Using a variety of marketing platforms will help you launch your product with maximum effect and reach a larger audience. The following are some channels to think about:

Social media: Use social media sites to interact with your audience, spread the word, and share updates. Create a content calendar and plan the postings that will occur before the launch. Urge your fans to disseminate the word and share.

Email marketing: Create a list of interested prospects and send updates and launch teasers to them on a regular basis. To encourage sign-ups, think about providing unique pricing or early access.

Public relations: Make contact with bloggers, influencers, and other media outlets to obtain coverage and reviews. Write a captivating press release and send it to industry journalists as a product pitch.

Paid Advertising: To reach a larger audience, think about putting targeted online advertisements on sites like Google Ads or social media networks. Create marketing efforts that accentuate the special qualities and advantages of your offering.

12.2.5 Involving Your Desired Readership
During a product launch, it's imperative to interact with your target market. Your goal is to pique their interest and motivate them to act. Here are some methods to keep your audience interested:

Interactive material: To engage your audience and entice them to share their product experiences, create interactive material in the form of giveaways, contests, and quizzes.

User-generated content: Ask your clients to use a certain hashtag when posting about their interactions with your product on social media. Repost and distribute their work to foster a sense of community and entice people to test your offering.

Limited-Time Offers: During the launch phase, instill a sense of urgency by providing exclusive offers or discounts that are only available for a short while. This can encourage prospective buyers to buy from you and take advantage of the exclusive offer.

12.2.6 Keeping an Eye on and Modifying Your Launch Plan

It's critical to keep an eye on the effectiveness of your launch plan throughout the product launch process and make any necessary revisions. Monitor important data, including visits to your website, interactions on social media, and sales conversions. Examine the data to find places where your plan needs to be optimized or improved. In order to guarantee a successful launch, pay attention to consumer feedback and make the required adjustments.

You may carry out an effective product launch that creates buzz, propels early sales, and lays the groundwork for your company's long-term success by adhering to these procedures and tactics. Don't forget to engage your target audience, create anticipation, create appealing messaging, use a variety of marketing channels, and constantly review and tweak your launch plan. Your product launch can be a big step toward building a profitable company if it is planned and carried out with care.

12.3 Acquiring Early Adoption and Clientele

Acquiring consumers and generating early traction are vital steps in developing a successful business after a successful product launch. This phase is essential since it lays the groundwork for the expansion and prosperity of your company. This section will discuss practical methods for drawing in and keeping clients in order to keep your business viable over the long run.

12.3.1 Identifying Who Your Target Market Is

Clearly defining your target demographic is crucial before implementing customer acquisition techniques. You may better target your marketing efforts and messaging to resonate with your ideal customers by knowing who they are. To determine the psychographics, behaviors, and demographics of your target market, conduct in-depth market research. With the use of this data, you will be able to develop marketing campaigns that are specifically targeted and will engage potential customers.

12.3.2 Creating a Powerful Brand Persona

Attracting and keeping clients requires a strong brand identity. Your mission, values, and unique selling proposition should all be communicated through your brand. Create a captivating brand narrative that connects with your target market and distinguishes you from the competition. Make sure that your website, social media accounts, and advertising efforts all convey the same message about your company. It will be simpler to attract and keep clients if you have a strong brand identity that inspires confidence in them.

12.3.3 Formulating a Marketing Plan for Multiple Channels

The implementation of a multi-channel marketing plan is crucial for achieving early traction and customer acquisition. By using a variety of channels to reach your target audience, this strategy raises your visibility and improves your chances of drawing in business. Think about combining digital marketing channels, including paid advertising, email marketing, content marketing, social media marketing, and search engine optimization (SEO). Every channel has advantages and might assist you in reaching various target audience segments. You may expand your audience and improve your chances of gaining clients by changing up your marketing strategies.

12.3.4 Making the Most of Influencer Marketing

Influencer marketing has become a potent instrument for attracting clients and building traction quickly. Find influential people that share your brand's values and have a sizable following in your industry or specialty. Work together to market your goods and services to their audience through these influencers. By using their already-established authority and trust, this tactic can help you raise awareness of your brand and draw in new clients. Make sure the influencers you select have a relevant and active following that fits in with your target market.

12.3.5 Putting Referral Programs into Action

Referral programs are a useful tool for word-of-mouth advertising to gain new clients. By providing awards, special access, or discounts, you can entice your current clients to recommend your goods and services to their friends, family, and coworkers. Through the utilization of personal recommendations, you may reach a larger pool of prospective clients who are more inclined to believe in and test your products. Putting in place a referral program benefits your business by bringing in new clients while also encouraging loyalty and fortifying ties with current ones.

12.3.6 Taking Part in Content Marketing

One effective tactic for drawing in and retaining potential clients is content marketing. Provide relevant, educational, and high-quality content that speaks to the issues and problems that your target audience faces. Post informational content on your sector or area, such as blog entries, articles, podcasts, films, and infographics, that offers answers and insights. You establish credibility in your industry and gain your audience's confidence by regularly producing insightful content. Because they will see the value in what you have to offer and be more willing to test your goods or services, your audience's trust can result in new customers.

12.3.7 Making Use of Social Media Promotion
Social media networks have strong advertising features that can efficiently assist you in reaching and gaining new clients. Make use of social media sites like YouTube, Facebook, Instagram, Twitter, LinkedIn, and so on to develop specialized advertising strategies. Utilize the sophisticated targeting features offered by the platforms to target a particular audience according to their geography, hobbies, habits, or demographics. Create enticing advertisement language and graphics that speak to your target market and encourage people to interact with your business. Make sure your social media advertising initiatives are consistently monitored and optimized for optimal efficacy and return on investment.

12.3.8 Delivering Outstanding Customer Service
Getting clients is only the first step; keeping them on board is just as crucial. Delivering

a remarkable customer experience is essential for retaining customers and generating word-of-mouth recommendations. Make sure your goods and services fulfill or go beyond the expectations of your clients. Provide rapid, individualized customer service to resolve any questions or problems. Put in place systems for collecting feedback from customers so you can learn from them and keep improving your services. When you put the needs of your consumers first, you'll attract devoted clients who will not only stick with your company but also promote it.

12.3.9 Examining and Improving Client Acquisition Techniques

You must constantly evaluate and improve your efforts if you want your client acquisition techniques to be as successful as possible. Keep an eye on important data, including conversion rates, return on investment (ROI), customer acquisition cost (CAC), and customer lifetime value (CLTV). To learn more about the effectiveness of your marketing channels and campaigns, use analytics tools. To maximize your efforts in acquiring new customers, pinpoint areas that require improvement and experiment with various approaches. You can hone your technique and get the most out of your outcomes by regularly evaluating and improving your strategies.

You may effectively attract clients and gain early traction by putting these methods and techniques into practice. Keep in mind that acquiring new customers is a continual process that calls for constant effort and modification. Maintain flexibility, keep an eye on market developments, and modify your plans as necessary to secure your company's long-term success.

12.4 Assessing and Modifying Your Launch Approach

An exciting and crucial step in your entrepreneurial path is launching a business. It's the result of many months or even years of careful planning, preparation, and hard labor. But this is just the beginning of the launch. After launching your company, it's critical to review and modify your launch plan to maintain ongoing success. This section will examine the significance of assessing your launch strategy and offer suggestions for any necessary modifications.

12.4.1 Evaluating Your Launch Strategy's Effectiveness

It's critical to evaluate the efficacy of your launch strategy before making any changes. By analyzing your launch plan, you can determine what was successful and what still needs work. The following crucial actions will assist you in determining how successful your launch plan was:

Examine important metrics and data.
Analyze the most important launch-related KPIs and data first. Metrics like website traffic, conversion rates, client reviews, and sales numbers are included in this. You may learn a lot about the effectiveness of your launch strategy and spot any areas that might need improvement by looking at these indicators.

Request client input
Consumer input is a priceless tool for assessing your launch plan. To find out what your customers think, reach out to them via social media, interviews, or polls. Inquire about their impression of your brand, their experience using your product or service, and any ideas they may have for improvement. You may learn a lot from this feedback about how well your launch plan connects with your target market.

Evaluate the market's reaction.
Analyze the reaction of the market to your debut by keeping an eye on market trends, rivalry among competitors, and consumer attitude. Are you making progress in the industry? Are buyers finding your goods or services satisfactory? Gaining insight into the market's reaction will enable you to evaluate the success of your launch plan and make any required modifications.

12.4.2 Modifying Your Launch Approach

It's time to make any necessary changes to your launch strategy after you've evaluated its efficacy. When adjusting, keep the following points in mind:

Identify and focus on the right audience.
You might need to adjust your target audience in light of the input and information you have received. Maybe you were a little off in your first assumptions about who your ideal client was, or you've found a new market that is more interested in your offering. You can better target your marketing efforts and improve your chances of success by making adjustments to your target audience.

Adjust your text.
Examine the message you employed for your launch to see if it successfully conveyed your value proposition and connected with your intended audience. Refine your messaging as needed to make sure it speaks to your customers' needs and pain points while also being true to your brand identity. In a crowded market, having a message that is both captivating and clear will help you stand out and draw in the ideal clients.

Make your marketing channels more effective.
Analyze your marketing channels' effectiveness to find out which ones are generating the most interaction and conversions. If some of your channels aren't working as well as they should,

think about shifting your resources to ones that are. Investigate fresh marketing avenues that complement the tastes and habits of your target market. You may reach a larger audience and get the most out of your marketing efforts by consistently tweaking your marketing channels.

Modify Your Approach to Pricing

A key factor in your company's success is pricing. Examine your pricing plan to see if it fits the perceived value and willingness to pay of your target market. Make any required price adjustments to make sure your offer is both profitable and competitive. Remember that setting prices is a continuous process that may involve revisions on a regular basis in response to consumer input and market conditions.

Improve your product or service through iterations.

The journey of your product or service doesn't end with its introduction. Iterate and improve continuously based on industry developments and client feedback. Determine what aspects of your product or service need improvement, then rank them. You may stand out from rivals and develop a devoted clientele by continuously providing value and attending to customer needs.

12.4.3 Tracking and Adjusting to Shifts in the Market

The business environment is always changing, so it's critical to keep an eye on it and adjust as necessary. Here are some crucial things to remember:

Keep abreast of industry trends.
Pay special attention to shifts in customer behavior, technology improvements, and industry trends. You can proactively spot business prospects and possible risks by keeping yourself informed. With this information, you'll be able to make wise choices and modify your launch plan as necessary.

Adopt a growth mentality.
Having a growth mentality is essential for being successful as an entrepreneur. Be receptive to criticism, flexible, and always looking for ways to get better. Having a growth mentality will enable you to modify your launch plan as needed to account for changes in the market.

Be nimble and adaptable.
Agility and adaptability are essential in the fast-paced commercial world of today. Should client tastes or market conditions change, be ready to adjust your strategy. This could entail finding new marketing outlets, improving your messaging, or changing your target demographic. Maintaining an advantage over competitors and securing the long-term prosperity of your company can be achieved by being adaptable and nimble.

In summary
A crucial stage in creating a profitable business

is assessing and modifying your launch plan. You may put your company in a position for sustained growth and success by evaluating the success of your plan, making the required modifications, and keeping an eye on developments in the market. Recall that starting a firm is simply the start of an exciting journey, and you can confidently navigate the always-shifting landscape of entrepreneurship with cautious assessment and change.